On the Fall of the Roman Republic

On the Fall of the Roman Republic

Lessons for the American People

Thomas E. Strunk

ANTHEM PRESS

Anthem Press
An imprint of Wimbledon Publishing Company
www.anthempress.com

This edition first published in UK and USA 2023
by ANTHEM PRESS
75–76 Blackfriars Road, London SE1 8HA, UK
or PO Box 9779, London SW19 7ZG, UK
and
244 Madison Ave #116, New York, NY 10016, USA

First published in the UK and USA by Anthem Press in 2022

Copyright © Thomas E. Strunk 2023

The author asserts the moral right to be identified as the author of this work.

All rights reserved. Without limiting the rights under copyright reserved above, no part of this publication may be reproduced, stored or introduced into a retrieval system, or transmitted, in any form or by any means (electronic, mechanical, photocopying, recording or otherwise), without the prior written permission of both the copyright owner and the above publisher of this book.

British Library Cataloguing-in-Publication Data
A catalogue record for this book is available from the British Library.

Library of Congress Control Number: 2021950922

ISBN-13: 978-1-83998-839-4 (Pbk)
ISBN-10: 1-83998-839-8 (Pbk)

Cover Image credit: Cincinnatus by Eleftherios Karkadoulias, 1988 –Sawyer Point Park, Cincinnati, Ohio, photo by Thomas E. Strunk, owned by the City of Cincinnati and used with permission of Cincinnati Parks.

This title is also available as an e-book.

*For Victoria and Sophia,
may they live in a nation of justice, freedom, equality and peace*

CONTENTS

Acknowledgments ix

Key Dates from Roman History xi

To the Reader xv

Introduction: Why Rome? 1

1 Anacyclosis: No Regime Is Exceptional and Democracy Is Not Inevitable 5

2 Mighty Republics Can Fall Because of Slow Corruption Rather Than Dramatic Revolutions 9

3 A Revered Tradition of Liberty Can Be Exploited by Authoritarians 13

4 Economic Inequality Drives Civil Strife 17

5 Political Violence Can Become Normalized 21

6 Strongmen Do Not Save Republics 27

7 The Rights and Responsibilities of Citizenship Need to Be Shared and Extended 33

8 Civic Virtue Is as Important as the Constitution and Laws 39

9 A Reckoning with the Oppressed Cannot Be Denied 45

10 Elections Only Work When Everyone Is Willing to Lose 49

11 Disregard for The Civil Liberties of Some Erodes the Legal Rights of All Citizens 53

12 Military Misadventures Abroad Lead to Instability at Home 57

13 Organized, Armed Gangs Tear Apart a Political System 61

14 Institutions May Not Be Able to Save the Republic 65

15 A Tyrant Backed into a Corner Is a Danger to the Republic 69

16 The Real Problem Is Not Simply a Tyrannical Leader	73
17 Free Speech Can Disappear	77
18 The Crisis Can Be Manufactured to Continue	81
19 The Revolution Can Be Advertised as a Restoration	85
20 Freedom Lost Cannot So Easily Be Regained	89
Conclusion	93
Notes	97
Bibliographic Note	125
Index	127

ACKNOWLEDGMENTS

The last two years have been a tumultuous time to write and publish a book. In that time, we have experienced a pandemic, economic instability, racial injustice, and a violent election season in the United States along with any number of smaller crises. Yet the tumultuous times provided the motivation and need to write this book rather than other books. To borrow from Brecht, the dark times will bring forth reflections on the darkness.

There has also been light. Light that has helped me complete this work. I would like to thank Megan Greiving and all those at Anthem Press who have helped produce this book. They have all been honest in their comments and timely in their assistance. I am especially grateful to the anonymous readers for their abundant and substantive comments. I would like to thank my colleague Graley Herren for recommending Anthem Press to me. I have shared this work with a number of kind readers who patiently provided their keen thoughts and fine writing insights on my clumsy rough drafts. In this respect, thanks are due to Brian Lavelle for his encouragement, the ever-patient James G. Keenan, Jonathan Zarecki, wise in the politics of the Roman Republic, and Ellen O'Gorman, whose timely visit to Cincinnati provided lively conversation on ancient Rome and modern politics. I would also like to thank Timothy Snyder, who encouraged me in this work. I have benefitted immensely from the wisdom from all those mentioned above; this book and any of its errors are all my own.

Thanks are also due to Don and Marlys Leslie, Tammy VanOrden, and Tom Strunk Jr., who keep me grounded in reality. The conversation, company and community of Ryan and Brandon Weaver, Rocky Fuller, JoAnne Davis, and Janet Martin have been greatly appreciated. I also need to acknowledge my debt and gratitude to Jamie, Victoria, and Sophia who provide me the joy to write and the time to do it.

KEY DATES FROM ROMAN HISTORY

BCE

753, April 21	Traditional date for founding of Rome; monarchy established
509	Traditional date for founding of the Roman Republic
458	Dictatorship of Cincinnatus
133	Kingdom of Pergamum bequeathed to Rome; Cornelius Scipio takes Numantia; tribunate and murder of Tiberius Gracchus;
123–121	Tribunates and murder of Gaius Gracchus
112	Jugurthine War begins
107	Marius elected consul for the first time
106	Jugurthine War concludes
104–100	Marius holds consulship consecutively
100	Saturninus and supporters murdered in the senate house
91	Tribunate and assassination of Marcus Livius Drusus
91–88	Social War
88	Sulla marches on Rome for first time, then leaves for campaign against Mithridates
87	Cornelius Cinna and Marius take over Rome in Sulla's absence; Sulla's supporters massacred
86	Marius dies while serving as consul for seventh time; Sulla defeats armies of Mithridates in Greece
83	Sulla returns to Italy
82–81	Sulla marches on Rome a second time, institutes proscription, and becomes dictator
81–79	Sulla holds dictatorship and reforms political constitution
73–71	Uprising of Spartacus
70	First consulship of Pompey and Crassus
67	Passage of anti-bribery law; Pompey's successful command against Mediterranean pirates
66	Candidates for consulship prosecuted under anti-bribery law of 67; Pompey given command against Mithridates in East

- 64 *Collegia* outlawed
- 63 Consulship of Cicero; Catiline loses consular election; Catilinarian Conspiracy
- 60 Formation of First Triumvirate by Caesar, Crassus, and Pompey
- 59 Consulship of Caesar
- 58 Clodius holds tribunate, legalizes *collegia*, and exiles Cicero; Caesar begins Gallic War
- 57 Cicero recalled from exile
- 55 Second consulship of Pompey and Crassus; Caesar's command in Gaul renewed
- 54 Crassus leaves Rome for campaign against Parthia
- 53 Crassus defeated and killed at battle of Carrhae
- 52 Clodius killed in violent confrontation with Milo on Appian Way; in Rome senate house burned during subsequent rioting; Pompey elected sole consul
- 50 Senate votes for Caesar and Pompey to disband armies but decree is vetoed
- 49 Caesar crosses Rubicon initiating civil war
- 48 Caesar defeats Pompey at battle of Pharsalus; Pompey killed in Egypt
- 47 Caesar dictator for one year
- 46 Cato commits suicide at Utica following Caesar's victory at Thapsus; Caesar becomes dictator for 10 years
- 44 Caesar becomes dictator for life; Mark Antony offers Caesar a crown at the Lupercalia festival, assassination of Caesar
- 43 Consuls Hirtius and Pansa killed in battle of Mutina; Octavian's first consulship; Mark Antony, Marcus Lepidus, and Octavian form Second Triumvirate and institute proscription; Cicero assassinated
- 42 Octavian and Antony defeat Brutus and Cassius at battle of Philippi
- 40 Treaty of Brundisium between Second Triumvirate, marriage of Antony and Octavia
- 37 Marriage of Antony and Cleopatra
- 34 Donations of Alexandria
- 31 Octavian defeats Antony at battle of Actium
- 30 Antony and Cleopatra commit suicide
- 29 Octavian returns to Rome in triumph
- 27 Octavian takes title of Augustus

CE

14	Augustus dies; Tiberius becomes emperor
25	Cremutius Cordus commits suicide following accusation of treason for his historical writings praising Brutus and Cassius
37–41	Caligula emperor
54–68	Nero emperor
81–96	Domitian emperor
212	Emperor Caracalla extends citizenship to the entire free population within the bounds of the Roman Empire
476	Traditional date for the fall of the Western Roman Empire

TO THE READER

When we speak of the fall of Rome, the modern imagination usually conjures the end of the Roman Empire[1] and Roman civilization in general sometime in the fifth or sixth century CE. This book is not about the fall of Rome, the end of the empire and a civilization, as popular thought would have it. It is not about barbarian hordes rushing over the border, cultural decadence or the effects of drinking from lead cups, or all the other fanciful notions of why the Roman Empire came to an end. This book is about how Rome went from being a kind of democratic society, the Roman Republic specifically, to an authoritarian and autocratic society—the Roman Empire. Rome would last another 500 years after the fall of the Roman Republic. The final collapse of Rome is a fascinating period to study and much more complex than the casual observer imagines, but that is the topic for another scholar and another book, many of which have already been written, beginning with Edward Gibbon's *The Decline and Fall of the Roman Empire*. The events covered in this book are not about dramatic ends, but about subtle shifts, which might not have been fully perceptible even to those living through them. This book's first concern is the transition from republic to autocracy and the rise of violence and authoritarianism that brought down the Roman Republic and which represents a significant threat to the republic of the United States.

A few points to start. Following the Introduction, I will begin with several introductory chapters (1–4), focusing respectively on the rise and fall of states and exceptionalism, slow corruption, liberty, and economic inequality. These four chapters explore some underlying ideas and concerns in Roman and American society while also providing the reader with some background information on Roman traditions and governance. Beginning with Chapter 5, I will be proceeding chronologically through Roman history from 133 BCE to roughly 27 BCE. I have made this choice to give the reader who is unfamiliar with Roman history a kind of narrative of the fall of the Roman Republic. Throughout this narrative, I will be mentioning change quite frequently in a negative sense. I do not mean to convey the idea that change is bad or that the Romans were never able to adapt in positive and constructive ways—change and adaptation are often necessary and productive—but a hallmark of the fall of the Roman Republic was the transgression of accepted political norms that had once preserved the Roman political system. The contravention of these norms initially represented exceptions, and then these exceptions became precedents to shape new norms antithetical to republicanism. In addition, I will write of the Roman constitution; this was not a written constitution like the US Constitution. The Roman constitution was a collective sense of the norms of political behavior and the individual laws the Romans passed in an attempt to enforce that political behavior.[2]

We typically describe the United States as a democracy; in casual usage this is fine, but more precisely, the United States is a republic. Like the Roman Republic, the citizens of the United States elect representatives to serve and make decisions on their behalf.[3] In a pure democracy, such as classical Athens, the citizens vote directly on laws and collective political action, and political offices are frequently determined by lot. Direct democracy may sound appealing to those disillusioned with our elected politicians, and it may very well be a preferable option, but republican forms of government have their virtues too. Most of all is the sense of service that is required for a successful republic. Ideally citizens seek office so that they can serve and represent their fellow citizens. Public service is a laudable ambition as it has the potential to call us beyond our own immediate self-interest, which can be a weakness of a direct democracy. The importance of public service requires a deep sense of the common good, which for republican forms of government represents more than an abstract idea; the word republic—Latin *res publica*—literally means "the public thing," "the common thing," or "the common good." For a republican form of government to function as it should, it needs by definition to have a robust sense of what serves the public good over private gain. The ancient Romans anchored their sense of the *res publica* in monuments to republican heroes, stories of sacrifice for the common good, such as Cloelia, Camillus, and Cincinnatus, and written documents and laws, such as the Twelve Tables and histories.[4] In the United States, our founding documents and subsequent important speeches and writings, such as the Declaration of Independence, the Seneca Falls Declaration of Sentiments, the Gettysburg Address, Martin Luther King Jr.'s "I Have a Dream" speech, and the Port Huron Statement, help us anchor our actions and behaviors in the common good.[5] We often do not live up to the aspirations these documents and speeches call us to, but they provide a compass that points the way to a more just and free society. In addition, we may visit museums or travel to the National Mall in Washington, DC, or to other historic sites and national parks and from them gain a sense of our national purpose.

Much of what is written here is informed by the election, presidency, and electoral defeat of Donald Trump. Trump's presidency has shattered many American political norms and coarsened American civic life. Whatever the future of Donald Trump and Trumpism, the forces that catapulted him to power have deep roots in American society and will not fade away simply because Trump was the loser of the 2020 US presidential election. Trump like many political leaders is as much the product of a movement as he is the inspiration for a movement. Although Trump currently maintains his grip on the GOP, it may be that Trump will fade from the limelight, but the United States should remain concerned with imitators of Trump. In many ways, he is a case study for citizens, scholars and politicians of what an authoritarian leader can achieve in American politics, and thus it is important to examine the period of his ascendency. It should also be pointed out that this study is not interested in identifying Trump with any particular Roman.[6]

In this book, I have adopted an ethos of brevity and simplicity. This choice comes with some risk since the topics discussed here for both ancient Rome and the modern United States are quite complex. I have aimed for a readable and accessible text, but the reader should assume a lengthy bibliography of scholarly and journalistic conversation, if not political controversy, on most topics. I have made reference in the notes to recent and significant works when relevant. Some particularly important ancient and modern works are listed in the Bibliographic Note.

Lastly, I write from the perspective that Roman history has lessons to teach us. Antiquity is not merely a fossil to be preserved on a museum shelf, but a tool to think with. Moreover, it is the duty of the historian to impart their knowledge and to reflect on its implications for the present. In what follows, I will present what I believe are the most significant lessons from the fall of the Roman Republic for our present time and place, the third decade of twenty-first century America. These are not simply comparisons suggesting that history repeats itself in some programmatic way; it does not. History is not inevitable or predictable. Inevitability is a totalitarian concept used to inhibit freedom of action, and predictions are for the weather. The past has the ability to offer us something more—lessons from which we can learn and make choices similar to or different from those in comparable circumstances in the past. History provides us knowledge and freedom to act with context and depth.

INTRODUCTION: WHY ROME?

At first glance, there may seem to be little reason for citizens[1] of the United States in the twenty-first century to look back to ancient Rome for political guidance. Of course, we know that ancient Rome had a profound influence on the Founders of the United States, and we can also see its inspiration if we walk around a city like Washington, DC, and look at the classical façades on many of the public buildings. We may also know that Rome had a mighty empire. Yet it is also well known that Rome was a violent, patriarchal, enslaving society. Women did not have the right of direct political participation; slavery was an unquestioned fact of life. Such realities should never be overlooked; although we may admire features of ancient Rome, we do not want to romanticize the Romans. We are not the Romans, nor should we want to become the Romans.[2] So this leaves us with a question: while such a society might have appealed to the Founders, what can ancient Rome possibly teach us, who claim to be so far beyond gladiatorial spectacles and slavery?

Well first, in a spirit of humility, we may want to admit that twenty-first century America is not so far advanced from such barbarisms. For example, more people are enslaved now through human trafficking than at any other time in human history.[3] Recognizing our own limitations also allows us to acknowledge that there are some things the Romans cannot teach us, or at least are not best suited to teach us. After all, for their many faults the Romans did not have the atomic bombs and internment camps that we have employed with such precision and efficiency. If we are looking for ways to avoid ethnic, religious, and racial hatred as well as the violence and genocide they can inspire, then the twentieth century is our master teacher. To this list, we can add America's genocide of indigenous peoples and the institution of slavery and its perduring effects on racial injustice.[4] Given America's racial tensions, studying antisemitism in Europe or our own history of white supremacy will most reward our studies.

Yet if we are also concerned, and I believe we should be, with the rise of political violence, authoritarianism, and the maintenance of our republic, then Rome is still our best teacher. Stalin's Russia is not the place to look to understand how a strong republic can devolve into an autocracy; Russia had a millennium of princes and czars before Stalin, not elected representatives. The rise of Hitler and the Nazi Party is instructive, but the Weimar Republic makes it into the history books primarily because of its short life and spectacular incompetence. Similarly, many contemporary analogues, such as Hugo Chavez's Venezuela, do not have centuries of republican governance. While no doubt there is much to learn from studying these other states, the Romans, however, are valuable teachers for us because of both the endurance of their civilization and the evolution of their political institutions over that time. Moreover, while the Western world has examples of other long-standing republics, such as Switzerland, Iceland, or Italian city-states like Florence and Venice, Rome and the United States share certain "personality" traits unlike these more insular republics, such as a very outward looking and expansionist spirit while at the same time experiencing the influence of others by virtue of being an open society. Just as the United States has styled itself a melting pot and a land of immigrants, so all roads led to (not from) Rome. The period that historians generally label the Late Roman Republic (133–31 BCE) was a time when Rome was a hegemonic power in the Mediterranean; the Republic was at its zenith. History will need to interpret when the republic of the United States reached its height, but certainly following the Second World War the United States has enjoyed near hegemonic status on the world stage.

Rome was founded as a monarchy on April 21, 753 BCE, as tradition has it. Kings held sway for 244 years and ruled rather effectively during that time until Tarquinius Superbus (the Arrogant), Rome's last king and a model tyrant, was driven out. After Tarquinius's son violently raped Lucretia, the wife of a leading citizen, the Roman people, led by Lucius Brutus (the Liberator), drove out the kings and established a republic in 509 BCE.[5] If this sounds familiar—a monarchy descended into tyranny overthrown and replaced with a republic—it should. We can see the same process at work in US history. Just as the Romans, we have experienced tyranny and had the courage to stand up against it to create a representative form of government, a struggle to perfect our union that continues to this day. The Roman Republic endured for 460 years from 509 BCE until 42 BCE—nearly twice as long as the United States has existed as a country—and for most of those 460 years, year in and year out, the Romans held elections, and took votes, and campaigned, and freely argued for the best course of action. Yet after 460 years of republican traditions, the Roman Republic came violently and yet almost imperceptibly to an end and was replaced by an autocratic form of government. So if we want to learn how authoritarianism can creep into a political system designed to maintain liberty, how rampant economic inequality can eat away at a highly functioning republic, and how political violence can tear apart a people who once had a robust sense of the common good, then Rome has much to teach the United States.

While the Romans have many lessons to offer us, I want to focus on four constellations that represent the most significant things the fall of the Roman Republic has to teach us at this time. They are the importance of civic virtue, the dangers of political violence, the inability of institutions to save a corrupt political system, and lastly the finality of the loss of freedom. Though not presented in this sequence, each lesson typically will touch upon one of these four areas. The next four chapters will provide some background to set the scene for Rome in 133 BCE.

Chapter 1

ANACYCLOSIS: NO REGIME IS EXCEPTIONAL AND DEMOCRACY IS NOT INEVITABLE

After centuries of general political stability, it is easy to imagine a sense of inevitability setting in; just as the seasons changed, so the Romans had their elections year after year, decade after decade, century after century. The Roman Republic with unusual regularity held elections, took votes, went to war, and passed laws. To be sure, there were disruptions occasionally—there were lawmakers and magistrates who overstayed their welcome; there was political strife, but as Tacitus writes, none of these lasted long and the Republic rolled on.[1]

Until the Republic came to a sudden end and became an autocratic system ruled by one man, which modern historians refer to as the Roman Empire. Yet the Republic did not collapse all at once. There was a century of intermittent civil strife (roughly 133–31 BCE), which culminated in two decades of bloody civil war (49–31 BCE). At the end of the civil wars, Octavian, the adopted son of Julius Caesar, emerged victorious. He quickly assumed the name Augustus, The-August-One, and became Rome's first emperor.

Four hundred and sixty years are a pretty good run, and we may be just as inclined to ask why the Roman Republic lasted so long as to ask why it finally fell. Even in antiquity, Rome's success was a topic of reflection. The Greek historian and politician Polybius (202–120 BCE) wrote an entire history in an attempt to understand how Rome grew from a relatively powerful city in Italy to a Mediterranean-wide empire in such a short time—less than a hundred years.[2] Polybius wrote at the height of the Republic and died just as it was seeing the first pangs of political tumult. He came to Rome as a high-profile political exile and became an astute observer of the Roman system. As a Greek, he brought an outsider's perceptivity and a knowledge of political theory.

In his search to understand Rome's success, Polybius found the answer in Rome's political institutions. Greek political theorists, beginning with Plato and Aristotle, had delineated the basic forms of political constitutions—monarchy, aristocracy, and democracy—and judged that the most durable and just constitution was one that mixed the best parts of each.[3] In Rome, Polybius found in reality what had previously existed only in theory—a "mixed constitution." He lays out how Rome combined elements from each constitution in its Republic.[4] The chief elected officials in Rome were the consuls; two were elected every year and held office for only one year. The consuls carried out the highest executive functions of the state—leading the armies, calling meetings of the senate and assemblies, and generally keeping order in the city. Polybius saw in the consuls the remnants of the kingly executive power.

The Roman senate, which was not an elected office but a council of elders, was the repository of collective memory and experience; its primary role was to advise the consuls and other elected magistrates. After a high-ranking magistrate completed his term in office, he took up his position in the senate to advise the newly elected officials. In this capacity, the senate oversaw Rome's foreign affairs and its treasury. For Polybius, the senate represented the element of the aristocratic constitution by continuing to give a role to its most experienced citizens (and generally its wealthiest). The senate could pass nonbinding decrees, but it could not make laws. The Roman people alone had the sovereignty to pass laws in their several assemblies. Certainly, the senate would advise the elected officials who proposed the laws to the assemblies, but the Roman citizenry would have to vote on any proposal hoping to have the force of law. Moreover, the assemblies elected the magistrates. For these reasons, Polybius conceived of the Roman people as the democratic element in Rome's constitution.

The strength of this mixed constitution, as Polybius saw it, resided in the checks and balances each part placed upon the other. The Roman magistrates had to court the people to be elected and then were expected to consult the senate and had to win the approval of the people to pass anything into law. The senate could not pass laws nor carry them out, but it did have great experience and authority to influence domestic and foreign policy. The people could only pass proposals that had been brought before them and had to defer to the power of public officials once they were elected, as well as give up their time to serve in the military under the command of these same magistrates.

It is important to note, however, that Polybius concludes his account of Rome's mixed constitution with a discussion of the inevitable decline of all political constitutions, including even the Roman Republic.[5] He calls this cycle of the rise and fall of constitutions *anacyclosis*, an obscure word these days to be sure, but one worth keeping in mind. In what seems to be a direct warning to Rome, Polybius writes that when a form of government is at its height, its wealth will create fierce rivalry and excessive competition for office and the other rewards of civic life, which will in turn lead to economic inequality, political violence, and the end of the political system. For the Romans and for the United States, Polybius provides a reminder that no system is exceptional. Political institutions and systems of checks and balances will only last so long and endure so much pressure before they decline or break entirely. Some constitutions will endure longer than others, but in the midst of civil strife, institutions can only do so much. Institutions and checks and balances are only as strong as the civic virtue of the citizens that uphold them.

Despite the checks and balances built into the Roman Republic, there was one grave weakness—the Romans had no check or balance for partisanship and factions. Although the Roman Republic did not have formal political parties as the United States does, the Late Republic did not lack strife and factionalism, which Roman historians viewed as a late development in Roman politics.[6] There was little the senate could do if a majority of the people and a magistrate united to form a faction. Moreover, the senate and magistrates could collude to manipulate the assemblies. This is to say that factions in Rome did not always line up with the system of checks and balances. Individual Roman citizens did not always view themselves acting collectively to preserve the power of the Roman people (*populus Romanus*). Moreover, Roman public officials did not always see themselves as working in solidarity with other magistrates to check the power of the Roman people or senate. Romans— senators, magistrates, and people—often found themselves, especially in the Late Republic (133–31 BCE), belonging to factions that ran athwart the system of checks and balances. For Rome, in the end, the monarchical power would win out over the democratic and aristocratic centers of power despite ongoing senatorial and popular assertions of power.[7] The senate was placated by honors and public recognition, and the people were satisfied with games, bread, and security; in exchange, they handed over their power and freedom to the emperor.

Although structured differently, the United States has a constitution designed with checks and balances, backed up with heavy doses of claims to exceptionalism. As all American school kids learn, the three branches of government—executive, legislative, and judicial— have ways of limiting the power of the other branches. The United States also has formal political parties, which are always involved in low-level strife with each other, but also tend to a conservatism that checks the extremes.[8] Yet like the Romans, the United States too has a great weakness in its constitution—there is no way to prevent partisanship from crossing the branches of government. There is an assumption in the US Constitution that the executive, legislative, and judicial branches have an inherent interest, adversarial even, in limiting the power of the other branches. This assumption is false. The primary political allegiance of most US politicians and citizens is to a political party, Democrat or Republican; loyalty to government branch is at best secondary. When the majority party in Congress is of the same party as the president, there is no inherent interest in checking the power of the president; one could argue that there is an inherent self-interest in enabling the president. Moreover, there is the potential for the political parties to devolve into factions within themselves, thus debilitating their proper civic functions. One can reasonably argue that the Republican Party in its current disposition has abdicated its customary functions in order to placate Donald Trump and his grievances over losing the 2020 election.[9]

When times are good, or there is an outside enemy to rally against, we tend not to worry much about the danger posed to the Constitution by hyper-partisanship. We presume that our Constitution and democracy will persist. And we treat it as something taken for granted, expecting pieces of paper to save us from our excesses and incivilities. Yet the Romans teach us that civil strife and factionalism have the very real ability to erode political institutions along with the checks and balances built into those institutions until the entire constitutional edifice is at risk of collapsing. Just as there was nothing inevitable about the continued existence of the Roman Republic, so there is nothing inevitable about the survival of the republic of the United States to exempt it from Polybius' law of *anacyclosis*.

Chapter 2

MIGHTY REPUBLICS CAN FALL BECAUSE OF SLOW CORRUPTION RATHER THAN DRAMATIC REVOLUTIONS

An account of the fall of the Roman Republic does not record the events of a day, a few months, a year, or even a decade. The history of the fall of the Roman Republic covers over a hundred years of political events. The Roman Republic, as Polybius had recognized, was certainly a durable form. It was not going to be toppled by a single coup or spontaneous riot. Indeed, ancient Rome had many dramatic moments in its history—just read the histories of Livy, Sallust, Tacitus, or Polybius. But ancient Rome also had stability. Centuries of political stability, in which the Romans built up political customs and civic traditions—the honored *mos maiorum* (the tradition of the ancestors). The fall of the Roman Republic is in many ways the story of how the Romans strayed from these customs little by little and failed to create solutions to perennial problems, while too frequently pursuing private gain rather than the common good.

The political upheaval that resulted in the fall of the Roman Republic began in 133 BCE with the murder of the tribune Tiberius Gracchus, about whom more will be said in Chapter 5. Though his murder was a dramatic event that left a strong impression among those who lived through it, the event itself at the time probably did not feel like a harbinger of the end of the Roman political system. In some ways, it was one event that could be isolated in time. Yet it was a watershed event because it changed the idea of what was acceptable in Roman political life, specifically the use of violence. This change in how the Romans related to one another resulted in further violence and greater transgression of the accepted norms of political behavior, such as magistrates holding office for more than one year at a time, citizens rioting in the assemblies, and generals marching armies on Rome. The Romans had not done these things before, or if they had done them, they quickly found them unacceptable. After 133 BCE, the Romans would find such stark violations of their republican traditions increasingly acceptable. Yet each violation could be seen at the time merely as an exception to the norm rather than the new precedent it frequently became. Many examples of this process, transgression of accepted norm becoming later precedent, will be cited throughout the following chapters. To provide just one example of this process here, we could point to the consulship of Gnaeus Pompey in 70 BCE, which he held without serving in any of the prerequisite political offices; most Romans tolerated it as an exception for a particularly gifted and powerful young man.[1] Twenty-seven years later in 43 BCE, Octavian (the future Augustus) saw it as a precedent for him to be declared consul before holding any of the prerequisite political offices and at the unconstitutional age of 19.[2] Fortified by eight legions, Octavian had little trouble overcoming the senate's reticence.

I have chosen 42 BCE, when Brutus and Cassius were defeated at Philippi by Antony and Octavian, as the end of the Roman Republic, but scholars debate the exact end date. For while it became clear that the Roman Republic ceased to be a republic and morphed into the Roman Empire, there was no precise moment when this happened. One could argue for 49 BCE, 31 BCE, 27 BCE, or perhaps even another date, for there was no proclamation, no collective decision when the Romans chose to become an autocracy rather than a republic.

To a great extent, this confusion is the deliberate working of the first emperor Augustus (previously Octavian), who recognized that his surest path to power was by portraying himself as someone who was restoring something rather than heralding a revolution. Augustus did not declare that he was taking autocratic powers—though he did reveal it in subtle ways—instead he proclaimed that he was restoring the ancient republic. Even in his final account of his rule, the *Res Gestae*, Augustus asserted at the end of his life that he had handed back the republic to the senate and people of Rome.[3] The perceptive, and cynical, recognized the autocratic nature of his actions, but for most there was always a plausible explanation for any particular course of action undertaken by Augustus. If he had proclaimed that he was establishing an autocracy of which he would be the master, he would have met stiff resistance and received the kinds of threats that led to the assassination of Julius Caesar, his adoptive father. Augustus's transformation of the Roman constitution was so skillful that many rejected the idea that anything had changed, but Tacitus, an astute historian of Roman politics, writes that although the public officials kept the same titles (consuls, tribunes, etc.), the state had undergone a revolution that had done away with the ancient customs and cast aside equality; all now looked to Augustus for their orders.[4]

Over the last several decades our country has witnessed exceptional events, which only accelerated under Donald Trump's presidency—increasing violence, contentious elections, the disappearance of accepted truth, and the transgression of political norms by our elected officials. For example, the unwillingness of the Republican-controlled Senate to hold hearings on President Obama's Supreme Court nominee Merrick Garland broke with a precedent dating back over a hundred years to Reconstruction; of course, the Republican-controlled Senate took the opposite approach under President Trump in confirming Amy Coney Barrett.[5] The increasing use of the filibuster by both parties prohibits even bipartisan legislation from passing the Senate. During the 2016 and 2020 presidential elections, former president Obama campaigned for candidates Clinton and Biden, a practice that previous former presidents had eschewed.[6] The United States has also seen dramatic events, such as the storming of the Capitol on January 6, which will be discussed in later chapters.[7] Yet while January 6 was unprecedented in many ways, there were antecedent assaults on federal buildings dating well before Donald Trump came along, such as Timothy McVeigh's bombing of the Federal Building in Oklahoma City in 1995.[8] We can choose to see these events as isolated incidents without coherence, but I want to suggest that they are connected events and markers of increasing corruption, civil strife, authoritarianism, and the breakdown of civic virtue. The fall of the Roman Republic demonstrates how a country can drift from democracy to authoritarianism without a clear demarcation of the transition. Most Romans did not realize that they were living in the Late Republic. In order to avoid living in a late republic, American citizens need to preserve the best of their institutions and renew their political norms. A constantly relevant question for citizens of a democratic republic is whether their political tendencies are expanding and strengthening its institutions and practices or weakening and corrupting them.

Chapter 3

A REVERED TRADITION OF LIBERTY CAN BE EXPLOITED BY AUTHORITARIANS

Like modern Americans, the Romans had a firm belief in liberty and a long-held hatred of tyranny. We are told they despised the word *rex* (king).[1] Hatred of tyranny makes a lot of sense for a people who overthrew an oppressive authoritarian monarch. What makes less sense is that after centuries of republican government such people would tolerate the restoration of autocracy.

The Romans understood liberty (*libertas*) most basically to mean the opposite of servitude.[2] If one was free, one was not enslaved. But this could also be stated another way—to be free meant not to have a master; and this definition can take on a broader metaphorical meaning when applied to the relationship between free citizens. The liberty of the Republic surely insisted on the idea that citizens were free from masters, but it also insisted that they were not free from each other. For the Romans, liberty meant being a free citizen in a community of other free citizens, such was the political system they set up when they drove out the last king. Liberty was a virtuous mean between the extremes of servility and flattery on the one hand and unrestrained dominance and license on the other.[3] An individual could fall out of this mean in one of two ways. Oftentimes, the powerful were attracted to the strong form of freedom, which the Romans called domination (*dominatio*) or license (*licentia*), individual power which we often mistake as true freedom. License culminated in a behavior that sought to master and dominate one's fellow citizens by seeking for oneself freedom from all public constraint. Ambitious citizens looking to accrue enough political power for themselves to make themselves a master (*dominus*) over their fellow citizens became tyrannical, but the Republic, when healthy, found ways either to subdue this type of citizen or to create a more productive outlet for them that worked for the common good.

The other extreme for a citizen was to be drawn to the weak form of liberty, that is freely choosing servility (*servitus*) and flattery (*adulatio*) rather than liberty and its responsibilities. Such a citizen ostensibly made the free choice to enable the domineering citizen in order to receive short-term benefits. Such an exchange required the servitude of the enabling citizen. As Publilius Syrus, a Late Republican author of moral sayings, wrote, "To receive a benefit (*beneficium*) is to sell your freedom (*libertas*)."[4] In the end, servile citizens surrendered their own freedom and became more like subjects than fellow citizens. The healthy republic could absorb such flattery and servile behavior, but in the end, servility enabled autocrats to overthrow the Republic.

The Romans had built checks and balances into the political system to maintain an equilibrium and overcome the common practice of seeking excessive power or benefits. The election of magistrates for only a one-year term is an example of this. There were obvious drawbacks to this arrangement, such as holding elections for every office every year. It was difficult to get experience and make institutional change before one's term of office was over. The Romans, however, were little concerned with experience in office, which they sought elsewhere in the lifetime appointments to the senate and the sovereignty of the people, or with institutional change, which they typically did not seek since they were out to preserve the system they had created. The Romans also believed firmly in the idea of the collegiality of office-holders, that is, every elected office had at least two occupants, if not more. The reasoning behind these two principles—annual elections and collegiality—was to prevent the accumulation of power in one person's hands. The system was designed to prevent an autocrat from gaining power. The Romans wanted no more kings. They wanted to be free of masters and to have political liberty grounded in the common good as they understood it.

In such a system and political community, liberty was an unquestioned good regardless of one's political opinions. Therefore, everyone rhetorically appealed to liberty as the underpinning of their political beliefs and motivations. At the end of the Republic, claims to liberty by competing factions were made at a fevered pitch. Caesar marched on Rome under the pretext of the freedom of the tribunes. His rivals resisted in the name of freedom against tyranny. Cassius and Brutus assassinated Caesar to wrest liberty from a tyrant as made clear from the coins they minted depicting the freedman's cap flanked by daggers. Augustus, Caesar's adopted son, avenged Caesar's death to restore liberty and the Republic. Liberty was always the pretext. Tacitus tells us that domination and autocracy are never established without appeal to liberty.[5] Therefore, citizens in ancient Rome needed to discern not simply who appealed to liberty and who did not, but rather who worked for the common good and fostered liberty for other citizens, and who merely employed the rhetoric of liberty to bolster their own claim to power.[6] Modern Americans need to be equally discerning.

Plato wrote that democracy most naturally degenerates into tyranny when its freedom becomes excessive.[7] This formulation is not a law of history by any means, but it is what happened to the Romans as the democratic parts of its government faded and an autocrat usurped its authority. Whether or not this will be the fate of the United States is unknown. The United States has its own complex history of liberty.[8] The Founders, who were greatly influenced by classical antiquity, generally did not see a conflict between freedom from monarchical oppression and the enslavement of other humans. If they did see a conflict, it did not prohibit them from agreeing to a constitution that narrowly defined freedom in practice as the possession of White, male landowners. Left out of the Constitution's most important rights were women, the enslaved, poor Whites, Native Americans, and immigrants. Much of American history can be read as an extension of these narrow rights to those who have been left out. With much struggle and bloodshed, the rights of White male landowners have been extended through the Civil War and subsequent amendments, the women's rights movement, the labor movement, the civil rights movement, and so on. Although all these liberation movements have taken collective action, Americans have rightly earned a reputation for excessive individual freedom, often demonstrated as a backlash against collective movements for expanding political rights. In fact, we can legitimately ask whether Americans at this point have liberty or simply a highly functioning form of individualism. If liberty can only occur in a free political community grounded in the common good and balanced between domination and license (excessive freedom) on the one hand and servile flattery (deficient freedom) on the other, then the COVID-19 pandemic has exposed a strong preference for rugged individualism rather than for a liberty that serves the community. The resistance to wearing a mask to protect against the virus is a strong indicator that Americans value the freedom of the individual over the liberty of the community. The lack of a communal sense of shared liberty has harmed the health of the American people and their political system.

The lesson is not to give up on liberty. Liberty, personal and national, is indispensable. It is rightly the foundational premise of all our national documents. We narrate our history as an expansion of freedom: the search for a more perfect union is in essence an attempt to perfect freedom. We too have expelled a tyrannical king. The United States has instituted checks and balances to prevent the accumulation of power in the hands of one or a few out of a deep concern for preserving freedom. Yet for that reason we need to be wary of those who would appeal to our emotions based on liberty. If authoritarianism comes to the United States, it will likely be couched in the rhetoric of liberty, not the language of servitude. After all, why would anyone support someone openly promising subjugation?

Yet autocrats and authoritarians are perfectly at ease with the rhetoric of liberty and eager to convince us that what they are trying to establish is our liberation rather than our servitude. So we must be vigilant not only for our freedom but also for the rhetorical appropriation of our liberty. We would do well to remember President Lincoln's words on maintaining the mean of liberty: "As I would not be a *slave*, so I would not be a *master*. This expresses my idea of democracy. Whatever differs from this, to the extent of the difference, is no democracy."[9]

Chapter 4

ECONOMIC INEQUALITY DRIVES CIVIL STRIFE

Although the city of Rome began as a poor community on the hills along the Tiber River, its slow but steady domination of the Italian Peninsula and its rather swift conquest of the Mediterranean made Rome immensely wealthy. The territories acquired in Spain, North Africa, and Greece within 70 years (202–133 BCE) had thrust upon Rome a fortune that it had little time to understand or to incorporate.[1] Moreover, the absence of any foreign foe of any magnitude put Rome in an unprecedented space. A generation or two before, Rome had been but one of several powerful Mediterranean states, but by 133 BCE Rome was the master of the Mediterranean, even if it did not control and occupy the entire land mass. The Romans had some breathing room and some time to ponder the new landscape, which would be an idyllic way to put it. Another way to put it is that Rome could no longer ignore the domestic concerns that had developed out of this rapid conquest and infusion of wealth. How would they do? Well, as it turned out, the Romans themselves accomplished what the Greeks and Carthaginians could not do: they brought down the Roman Republic.

The Romans had always thought of themselves as simple agricultural people. Even if the stories of early Romans were over-romanticized, there is no question that the Romans included in their legal code the restriction of certain kinds of ostentatious displays of wealth. The Twelve Tables, Rome's earliest code of laws, restricted the conspicuous display of wealth at funerals. Subsequent laws sought to address public luxury and opulence in other areas, such as the amount of money spent on entertainment and banquets.[2] Why did the Romans pass these laws? A cynical, though accurate, view would be that people must have been conspicuously displaying their personal wealth. But why did the Romans think that was a bad thing? In modern capitalist countries, such public displays of one's personal wealth are often considered a virtue, whether they truly are or not. The Romans, however, understood the capacity wealth had to tear the state apart. First, luxury had the power to seduce citizens to pursue private wealth over the common good and then to use that wealth to consolidate political power. Second, the acquisition of great wealth by some citizens could result in alienation and civil strife when those without private wealth saw that the spoils of war and conquest were not being evenly distributed despite the entire community's contribution of blood, sweat, and toil to acquire them.

Roman historians, such as Livy, Polybius, and Sallust attributed the decline of such traditional virtues to the desire and pursuit of private wealth that had now become possible through the expansion of the empire.[3] By 133 BCE, the seductive power of wealth and personal luxury began to erode the civic virtue taught in stories and codified in law. The success of the Roman military had created an unforeseen negative side effect. The victorious Roman armies brought back immense wealth, much of which found its way into the hands of the elites.[4] Moreover, the Italian countryside experienced a population boom resulting in family farms being divided into smaller and smaller parcels for each male child. Some parcels were so small that their owners fell below the property requirements for military service.[5] This compelled many Roman landowners to sell their land to wealthy elites, who consequently gobbled up much of the land in the countryside. Thus, many Roman landowners were dispossessed of their land and their means of livelihood and had to look elsewhere for economic opportunities, which they found only with great difficulty in the city. Moreover, wealthy landowners frequently did not employ Romans to work the fields; they now used their immense wealth to stitch together large estates throughout the countryside and exploited enslaved labor to work the land.[6] Rome had long enslaved people, but for most of the Republic it did not have the wealth to be a slave society; its Mediterranean conquests changed that.

The last 100 years of the Roman Republic in many ways tell the story of how wealth and luxury drove personal political decisions and civil strife.[7] Many Roman citizens felt alienated and left out from the prosperity they saw around them. Politicians played off these divisions for personal gain and advancement. Sallust writes that for all parties, wealth was more important than virtue; in sum, everything was for sale in Rome.[8] Those who attempted to address these now endemic problems were met with great resistance and even violence, thus discouraging others from taking up the challenge of finding solutions that served the common good.

In the United States, economic inequality has been on the increase since the 1980s. Since the Great Recession of 2008, however, inequality has risen steeply, and the coronavirus pandemic has only exacerbated it.[9] The Gini coefficient, which measures income inequality, has risen steadily in the United States since the mid-1970s (0 being complete equality, 100 being complete inequality): in 1974 it was 35.3, and by 2018 it rose to 41.4 (the highest ever occurred in 2014 at 41.5).[10] The United States easily has the highest Gini coefficient of any G-7 nation.[11] Further, the CEO-to-employee pay ratio has ballooned at the 350 largest companies from 21-to-1 in 1965 to 320-to-1 in 2019 according to the Economic Policy Institute; a Harvard study put the 2020 ratio at 227-to-1.[12] The most conservative estimates, including all CEOs and based on hourly pay but not including benefits, puts the ratio around 6-to-1.[13] The rise in economic inequality coincides with the decline in union membership. In 1983, the union membership rate was 20.1 percent; by 2020, the union membership rate had dropped to 10.8 percent.[14] With the decline in union membership, there has been a decline in middle-class economic and political power. Much of the decline in union membership is the result of hostile government policy, which has increased the power of corporations.[15] In addition, union membership has also declined because middle and working-class workers have accepted the rhetoric of individualism over collective action. All these indicators suggest that economic inequality will continue to increase unless policies are adopted to reverse the trajectory and power is shifted to the middle-class and away from elites.

Economic inequality is not simply a problem for those citizens who have not participated in the economic recovery since 2008. Citizens who are left out from the economic prosperity of the rest of the country become alienated and are vulnerable to the seductions of racism, xenophobia, and resentment toward their fellow citizens. We should not be surprised to hear that many arrested for storming the Capitol on January 6 have a history of financial hardship.[16] Although financial hardship does not justify their violent actions, it does help to explain their motivations and the dangers of economic inequality. We want our fellow citizens to feel part of the political community and to make political decisions out of informed reflection, not the desperation that comes from unemployment, opioid addiction, or lack of health care. For if inequality is ignored or denied and reasonable demands, such as good jobs, quality health care, and affordable housing, are rejected, citizens will feel disaffected and begin to question why they should continue to support a system that does not support them. For example, when the Paycheck Protection Program was established during the early days of the economic crisis created by the pandemic, the funding was designated for small companies to continue to pay their employees, but this is not what happened; the majority of the funding went to large companies and even philanthropies. Many companies have continued to reap profits at the same time as they have laid off workers.[17]

It is easy, and perhaps necessary, to feel alienated from a government that tolerates and enables such corruption. This alienation creates a space for powerful and wealthy citizens to exploit the resulting resentment and to encourage radical means to be adopted, and likely in a way that does not help the poor but rather the politician who exploits the political divisions. The violence that brought down the Roman Republic did not result in the redistribution of wealth for the Roman people. The revolution did not deliver: the once powerful Roman people were bought off with bread and circuses and the political elite were left to indulge in flattery for benefits.[18] Economic inequality was largely the same before and after the fall of the Republic, but what was new was an autocracy that had used the divisions between citizens for its own establishment and now greatly limited the freedoms of poor and rich alike. We do not want to travel any further down this road to entrenched economic inequality than we already have. It will not lead to a flourishing democratic republic.

Chapter 5

POLITICAL VIOLENCE CAN BECOME NORMALIZED

The year 133 BCE should have been a year of great triumph for Rome. Scipio Aemilianus had taken Numantia, thereby solidifying Rome's control of central Spain (it had already subdued the southern and eastern portions). The same year, Attalus III, king of Pergamum in Asia Minor (modern-day western Turkey), bequeathed his wealthy kingdom to Rome; this was a gift of immense fortune that was acquired without a single casualty. Yet 133 BCE is typically not remembered for these auspicious events, instead 133 BCE is most remembered for being the year Tiberius Gracchus's body was found floating dead in the Tiber River along with the bodies of his political supporters.[1]

Tiberius Gracchus, a tribune of the plebs, and his adherents had been beaten to death on the Capitoline Hill, Rome's most sacred space. Despite the pleas of Gaius Gracchus, Tiberius's brother, the conservative faction of the senate which had incited the violence refused to surrender the body for burial. Adding to their abuse, they dragged the dead down to the riverside and threw their bodies into the Tiber, a final reminder of what would happen to those who defied their authority. Tiberius's murder was all the more vicious because as a tribune of the plebs his body was sacrosanct—to violate his body physically was a crime not only against a fellow citizen but also against the gods. For the first time under the Republic, not since the expulsion of the kings nearly four hundred years earlier, Romans decided that political violence was the answer to their disagreements.[2] No one involved in the events surrounding the murder of Tiberius Gracchus in 133 BCE could have understood the full ramifications of their actions. This act of political violence ushered in over one hundred years of strife, upheaval, and civil war until the centuries's old traditions of the Roman Republic yielded to the autocracy of the Roman Empire.

Tiberius Gracchus was from a prosperous Roman family that had demonstrated its competence and patriotism over several generations.[3] It was no surprise then that in 133 BCE Tiberius Gracchus was elected to the office of tribune of the plebs. Although the office was not the highest rung on the

Roman political ladder, the role of the ten annually elected tribunes of the plebs was to protect the common people of Rome; the office held immense power, including the right to call an assembly, to pass legislation, and to veto decrees of the senate and assemblies. Tiberius came to this office at a time when Rome could no longer ignore some of the pressing demands that had been lingering for a generation or two. Most acutely, the Romans were getting short on citizens who owned enough land to meet the property qualification to serve in the military—the thinking being that if one owned land, one had a vested interest in defending Rome and even further had the funds necessary to purchase military weapons and equipment.[4] Although Rome had fought many protracted and successful military campaigns abroad throughout the third and second centuries BCE, such as in Greece, North Africa, and Spain, Rome still did not have a professional standing army. Therefore, if Rome was to field armies, it would need more landowning citizens.

As tribune, Tiberius Gracchus had the idea that the solution to this problem was to grant land to Roman citizens. But where to find it? Over the centuries, as Rome conquered the Italian Peninsula, much of the land was taken over as the public property of Rome. As the land was lying fallow, however, many nearby landowners simply began to cultivate this public land. Tiberius Gracchus took the radical notion to redistribute this public land to the landless. Needless to say, this plan was controversial. Those who had been cultivating and profiting from the public lands resisted this redistribution. Tiberius got nowhere with his proposal in the senate, many of whose members were the wealthy landowners cultivating these public lands.[5]

The senate, however, did not respond to Tiberius's proposal with a counterproposal that would have addressed the dilemma Rome was now facing; rather than focusing on the common good, senators focused on maintaining their own power and wealth. Rebuffed by this traditional avenue of political debate and consultation, Tiberius Gracchus recognized and acted on the recognition that Roman elected officials did not have to consult the senate; it was merely a tradition. The assemblies of the Roman people were the sovereign legislative bodies, and Tiberius Gracchus was confident that they would support his legislation. So Tiberius Gracchus took the extraordinary measure of side-stepping the authority of the senate and went directly to the people; this act was not illegal, but it was a highly controversial move. The people passed the legislation, and a land commission was established and funded with the treasure of Attalus. This episode is an important example of the people and an elected official forming an alliance against the senate, which would become a common feature of the Late Republic. At the end of the year, Tiberius Gracchus sought reelection, something that was also highly discouraged. Though again not strictly illegal, Roman politicians did not typically seek reelection to the offices they just held, as this was a violation of the principle that one held office for only one year, a traditional check on the power of office-holders—there were no incumbents. This tradition is an example of what Levitsky and Ziblatt call forbearance, the practice of moderation in pursuing one's political agenda.[6] For example, prior to the passing of the Twenty-Second Amendment in 1947, US presidents could serve for more than two terms, but all of them, up until President Franklin Roosevelt in 1940, exercised forbearance in following George Washington's example of serving only two terms. Similarly for the Romans, custom and forbearance inhibited taking legislation directly to the people without senatorial approval or running for reelection, though there was no legal prohibition against it. These challenges to the senate's authority were too much for the Roman system to bear all at once. At the assembly in which the election was to be held, Tiberius Gracchus and hundreds of his supporters were attacked and murdered by a mob of senators. This massacre was the first political violence on such a large scale since the founding of the Republic.[7]

A decade later, Gaius Gracchus, Tiberius's brother, took up the mantle of the struggle and was elected tribune of the plebs for 123 BCE. Gaius introduced an ambitious legislative agenda, including among others restrictions against capital punishment, provisions for grain at a reduced price, extension of citizenship to the Italian allies, and expansion of land distribution.[8] Gaius passed much of his legislative agenda and succeeded in being reelected for 122 BCE. Gaius's reelection provides a good example of something that was once transgressive, his brother Tiberius's pursuit of a second consecutive term, becoming acceptable. In his second year in office, opposition stiffened against Gaius. His proposal to extend citizenship to Rome's Italian allies failed and would remain a sticking point in Roman politics for several more generations. Gaius sought a third term as tribune, but he did not win reelection. In 121 BCE, following an assembly that turned violent, the senate passed a Final Decree, the *Senatus Consultum Ultimum*, in essence a declaration of martial law, allowing for the consuls to use force and to kill Roman citizens without trial. This was the first time such a decree was passed. Over the course of the next century, the senate approved such decrees at times of civil strife, and their doubtful legality became a point of controversy. The consul Lucius Opimius, a fierce opponent of Gaius, organized a senatorial mob to attack Gaius and his supporters. In the ensuing violent conflict, Gaius Gracchus fled and committed suicide with the help of his servant; he was subsequently beheaded by his pursuers. Three thousand of his followers were slain, and as his brother before him, his body and those of his supporters were thrown into the Tiber River.[9]

Though the violence quickly ended in each instance—there were no corresponding retaliations—the murders of Tiberius and Gaius Gracchus were a loss of innocence for the Romans. From 133 BCE until the fall of the Republic, political violence once unleashed became a regular part of Roman politics. Roman political violence manifested itself in several ways. Sometimes, political violence resulted in the assassination of a political opponent, such as when the tribune Marcus Livius Drusus was assassinated in 91 BCE. Sometimes, there was mass violence, as when Gaius Marius and Cornelius Cinna massacred the supporters of Lucius Cornelius Sulla in 87 BCE. And at other times, there was even outright civil war, as in 83–82 BCE when Cornelius Sulla marched on Rome, defeated his opponents in pitched battle, declared himself dictator, and drew up a proscription list, all of which resulted in the deaths of thousands of Romans. Those on the proscription lists could be brutally murdered and their property confiscated, from which rewards were paid to the assassins.[10] The assassination of Tiberius Gracchus was merely the first instance and represented the violence of elites against the opposition who wanted reform. The other two types of violence, outright civil war with organized armies marshalled against each other and violence between citizens organized in gangs or quasi-paramilitary groups, I will discuss further in later chapters.

The last century of the Roman Republic was a legacy of violence. It had started as a response to the political reforms of Tiberius Gracchus and ended in outright war. The suffering was immense. Political violence became the way Romans addressed political problems. Once it had become an acceptable part of Roman life, the Romans were unable to imagine a way to stem it except through the power of an autocrat.

Democracy as a system, and each round of elections, is a kind of low-level civil strife. In the United States, political opponents hurl insults at each other, and citizens line up on either side of the political parties. People march for change, donate money to political organizations, and write their opinions in the press. There can be an ugliness to this political culture, but there is also something beautiful when democracies can engage in political wrangling with little to no violence. This low-level civil strife is a sign that democracy is at work; a society that outlaws and smothers opposition is a totalitarian regime. We want there to be loud, yet peaceful, voices in our political life. Such had been the case in Rome for almost four hundred years. Yet there is a line, which we do want to walk close to, but which we dare not cross, and that is the line between strong words spoken with conviction and violent acts that have been incited by hateful rhetoric.

Political violence has been a part of American history from its founding. The brutality visited upon the enslaved and indigenous peoples is the foremost example of a sustained practice of violence. The Jim Crow era regularly employed violence to limit the political rights of Black Americans for whom attempting to cast a ballot was a life-threatening endeavor. The Tulsa

Race Massacre of 1921 horrifically demonstrates the violent measures White Americans have been willing to take to assert their dominance in society.[11] The labor rights movement too was met with deadly resistance.[12] The Battle of Blair Mountain, also in 1921, saw thousands of miners and National Guard troops in open armed conflict.[13] It has been 100 years since the Tulsa Race Massacre and the Battle of Blair Mountain, and we still have not reckoned with the racism and economic inequality that triggered those events and that have plagued American society for so long. Until we do so, the threat of political violence will linger.

In recent years, we have seen individual citizens increasingly resort to political violence. The wide availability of assault weapons has made violence against fellow citizens easily possible and over the last decade more prevalent. Examples abound. In May 2017 on a streetcar in Portland, Jeremy Joseph Christian stabbed Micah Fletcher and murdered Ricky Best and Taliesin Namkai-Meche, all of whom intervened when Christian verbally attacked two young women, Destinee Mangum and Walia Mohamed, with racist and Islamophobic insults. James Fields killed Heather Hyer and injured others at the protests in Charlottesville on August 12, 2017. Patrick Crusius deliberately targeted Mexicans in his anti-immigrant attack in El Paso that killed 22 people on August 3, 2019. Asian Americans and Pacific Islanders have experienced increased violence culminating in the spa shootings in the Atlanta area by Robert Aaron Long that left eight people dead, six of whom were Asian.[14] Undoubtedly, by the time you are reading this, newer examples will be available. These acts have been accomplished by individuals acting on their own impulses, but there was enough firepower in Charlottesville to kill many people. Moreover, Trump as president encouraged such violence. At a campaign rally in Florida on May 9, 2019, the president, ostensibly there to give support to hurricane victims, asked those attending, "But how do you stop these people?" referring to migrants. A voice from the crowd shouted, "Shoot them!" Trump laughed and said, "Only in the Panhandle, you can get away with that statement. Only in the Panhandle!" The audience erupted in cheers.[15] The emotional fervor at Trump rallies has been a warning of the potential for organized violence, culminating in the unprecedented storming of the Capitol by a seditious mob at the president's command on January 6.[16] If we do not draw back from the line separating healthy democratic debate from outright violence, we may find, as the Romans did, that deadly violence will either become a customary part of political life or peace will come only with an autocrat who will put a stop not only to the violence but also to democratic republicanism.

Chapter 6
STRONGMEN DO NOT SAVE REPUBLICS

In the wake of the assassination of the Gracchi, which demonstrated that political reform through traditional means could be stymied or prevented through violence, Roman citizens and soldiers increasingly rallied around rich and powerful men, who used their great wealth and power to provide for their supporters. The close allegiance of soldiers to their military commanders degraded a shared sense of purpose among the Romans and allowed individuals to amass extraordinary power and influence. Moreover, the rivalries between these strongmen frequently led to conflict and violence between them and their partisans. It is easy for the history of the Late Republic to be a study simply of these "great men." All of them achieved some good things for Rome; all of them also either brought great destruction to Rome or paved the way to autocracy. At times, they exploited aristocratic sentiments, at others they played upon the emotions of the common people. They all profited personally whether their constituents did or not.

Gaius Marius was the first of Rome's strongmen of the Late Republic; others would follow—Sulla, Pompey, Caesar, and Augustus, all of whom will be discussed in subsequent chapters. Marius came from relatively humble origins. He started out as a new man (*novus homo*), a technical term indicating a politician who was the first of his family to attain the senate, or even more exclusively the first to reach the consulship. Although Marius did not have an aristocratic legacy, he did have ambition and talent, particularly military talent. Politically, he tended to favor popular measures, such as his bill in 119 BCE as tribune of the plebs to prevent voter intimidation in the assemblies, an example of a benefit he provided the political system.[1]

Marius rose to the forefront of Roman politics during the war with Jugurtha in North Africa, which broke out in 112 BCE.[2] Jugurtha showed himself a difficult opponent to defeat. Several rounds of generals failed to bring the war to completion. Marius had been serving in the war under the commander Quintus Metellus when he returned home to seek the consulship for 107 BCE, which he won in large part because of popular support.[3] In an example of the people's sovereignty and independence and the senate's weakening authority, the people chose Marius to take over the war against Jugurtha, although the senate had already decided to continue the command of Metellus, who had been making steady progress in the war. This reversal of the senate's appointment by the people was a rather unprecedented event, as typically the senate appointed provincial commanders. In the decades following, the people would overturn the senate's decision on several key appointments, granting extraordinary commands to the most popular military commanders, Gnaeus Pompey and Julius Caesar among them. But the nature of Marius's appointment was not the most innovative part of his agenda.

Marius astutely recognized that more troops were needed to complete the war against Jugurtha. As mentioned previously, Roman recruits were traditionally selected from the propertied classes; Marius overlooked this rule and called for volunteers from those who did not meet the property qualification, the *proletarii*.[4] Marius outfitted these men, who garnered the nickname "Marius's Mules" on account of the many weapons and supplies they carried, and in turn these men helped Marius win the war, but this precedent had far-reaching consequences. Indeed, Marius brought much-needed reforms to the military and did much to professionalize Rome's army, a process which would take another century to complete. Yet equally important, Marius owed his success to these soldiers, and they owed their newfound status as Roman soldiers to their commander rather than to the broader Republic. The army had become politicized. Upon release from service, these veterans received land grants through Marius's patronage. They would go on to cast the votes that led to Marius holding the consulship an unprecedented five years in a row (104–100 BCE).[5] Later Romans, such as Sulla, Pompey, and Caesar would court the personal allegiance of their troops to back up their political agendas with the force of the Roman legions.

Marius's supporters could justifiably argue that he achieved much good for Rome, such as his needed reforms of the military and his defeat of Rome's enemies. For his efforts Cicero called him the *conservator patriae*, preserver of the country; he was hailed as the new founder of Rome and put his own image on coins, the first time ever for a living person.[6] Yet in the end Marius served his own interests, not the common good. In an effort to get his veterans land, Marius allied with Lucius Appuleius Saturninus, a fiery tribune of the plebs, who in 103 BCE passed the legislation for Marius's veterans and supported him for another consecutive consulship, his third in a row and fourth overall. This alliance alone offers little controversy, but personal ambition rather than dignified retirement spurred Marius on to continued engagement in partisan politics and several more consecutive consulships, bringing his total to six. He maintained his support for Saturninus, who became only more radical in his tactics. In 100 BCE, Saturninus, again as tribune, passed another law providing land for veterans, but this time violence broke out in the assembly convened to vote on the legislation; Saturninus and his supporters held the field and passed the now controversial law.

In the consular elections of 100 BCE, Saturninus and Gaius Servilius Glaucia, an ally running for consul, used violence and killed a competing candidate by clubbing him to death. Riots ensued for several days as violence spread throughout the city. Once again, the senate passed a Final Decree authorizing the consul to take any necessary steps to protect the Republic; Marius was the consul. Marius chose to carry out the decree against his former allies, whom he gathered in the senate house to await trial. While they were being detained there, a mob climbed the roof and began hurling down the roof tiles, killing Saturninus, Glaucia, and their supporters, many of whom were holding office at the time. The senate house, one of Rome's greatest symbols of its republic, had become a murder scene. The violence continued for days.[7] By aligning himself with politicians who were willing to engage in violence, Marius had sown the wind; he was now reaping the whirlwind because he was unable to control them.

Although Marius faded from the political scene for the next decade following Saturninus's death, he had one final act, displaying most clearly Marius's personal ambitions. His desire to command the war against Mithridates, king of Pontus, led Marius to become involved in one of the first clashes of Roman soldiers in the city of Rome. In 88 BCE, the consul Sulla, a former lieutenant of Marius, though a political enemy, was appointed to govern the province of Asia and to oversee the looming war against Mithridates. As Sulla set out to meet his troops, Publius Sulpicius Rufus, a tribune friendly to Marius, proposed stripping Sulla of the command and appointing Marius in his place, a controversial move, nonetheless the assembly of the people ratified the proposal. Sulla was furious, and rather than surrender the command, he marched his army on Rome, the first time ever such a move had been taken in the existence of the Republic. Roman soldiers were traditionally not allowed in Rome and had to remain stationed outside the city. Sulla's attack on Rome was successful; he quickly took the city, and Marius and Sulpicius were declared, without a trial, outlaws and were forced to flee. Sulpicius was found and killed; Marius, however, survived, and once Sulla departed with his army for the East, he and his ally Cinna returned and took exacting vengeance on Sulla's supporters. For five days, Marius's supporters had their way in the city, murdering and looting; Marius's foremost political enemies were executed, including six former consuls. A few days after taking up the consulship for the seventh time, Marius died. Marius claimed to be a man of the people and he did accomplish great military deeds, but in the end, he also did great damage to the Republic. Sulla would return in due time from the East to exact his own revenge, but that is another lesson.[8]

Of late, we have seen the reemergence of strongmen around the globe—Vladimir Putin, Nicolás Maduro, Rodrigo Duterte, Recep Tayyip Erdogan, Narendra Modi, Viktor Orbán, and Donald Trump foremost among them.[9] Trump is not the first strongman to come along in American politics. Others who aspired to the role in some form include Huey P. Long and Richard Nixon.[10] We could argue over whether Trump is a strongman in the technical sense, which often suggests a strong military connection, something Trump has lacked.[11] Yet Trump has taken over the Republican Party, reducing it from a party that only recently had many voices and leaders, evidenced by the 2016 primary, to a party that hews very closely to the will of one man.

Moreover, Trump animated our politics with implied, if not direct, threats of violence. Thus, in 2016, candidate Trump proclaimed, "I could stand in the middle of Fifth Avenue and shoot somebody and I wouldn't lose any voters"—an astounding statement for a presidential candidate to suggest he could kill someone.[12] Trump's assertion was a time honored tactic by authoritarians—publicly state the possibility of an unprecedented act to see how the public responds; if outrage follows, then the statement was merely hypothetical and taken out of context; if complacency follows, then the way to action is cleared. Trump would indeed be complicit in at least seven deaths due to the storming of the Capitol on January 6, 2021.[13] To date, he has suffered little lasting consequence for inciting the attempted coup, aside from temporarily being banned from social media. Although more Republicans voted for Trump's second impeachment, the most ever from any president's own party in an impeachment trial, the majority of Trump's followers did indeed continue to support him at the local, state, and national levels.[14] So Trump was largely correct—he did not lose any voters following the deaths at the US Capitol. Although Trump lost the 2020 election, there is nothing to stop him or another future candidate or president of either party from acting with similar threats and violence.

Rome's strongmen—Marius, Sulla, Pompey, Caesar, and Augustus—all justified their actions on the grounds that extreme actions were needed and that they alone could save the Roman people.[15] In 2016, Trump made the same assertion when he accepted the Republican Party's nomination, proclaiming loudly, "I am your voice." He later added, "No one knows the system better than me, which is why I alone can fix it."[16] Such appeals to being uniquely qualified are standard fare for presidential candidates, but Trump's rhetoric made a claim for being a political savior. Unlike Marius, Trump has no military experience, however much he may want to project such an image. Until recently, the US military, despite whatever politics swirled around it, had remained largely unpoliticized. Yet Trump seized the opportunity to deploy the military during the Black Lives Matter protests in the wake of George Floyd's murder in the spring of 2020. In a speech in the White House Rose Garden on June 1, Trump said that he wanted to "dominate the streets" and described the protests as "acts of domestic terror."[17] Trump then used the military against US citizens and was joined by a chorus of lawmakers calling to invoke the Insurrection Act of 1807.[18] Soldiers surrounded the Lincoln Memorial and protesters were tear-gassed out of Lafayette Square, so Trump could pose with a Bible in front of the St. John's Episcopal Church. Former Defense Secretary James Mattis notably rebuked Trump for doing this, as did many other former military officers.[19]

Yet Trump, despite allegations that he called wounded, captured, and dead service members "suckers" and "losers," has also been supported vocally by retired generals and admirals who in September 2020 threatened that "our historic way of life is at stake" should Democrats continue to be elected.[20] Another letter published in May 2021 by Flag Officers 4 America stated, "Under a Democrat Congress and the Current Administration, our Country has taken a hard left turn toward Socialism and a Marxist form of tyrannical government which must be countered now by electing congressional and presidential candidates who will always act [*sic*] to defend our Constitutional Republic."[21] Though political endorsements by retired military members are neither new nor of themselves controversial—Biden had his military supporters too—the alarmist rhetoric of these letters should be startling. The difference between Trump, or any US president, and Rome's strongmen resides in their relationship with the military. Rome's strongmen, as consuls, were direct commanders of armies; although American presidents serve as commander in chief, nonetheless they do not directly command the military. Generals and admirals do, and they must remain independent from political partisanship. As the Late Republic teaches us, the independence of the military is an absolute must for a democratic republic.

Chapter 7

THE RIGHTS AND RESPONSIBILITIES OF CITIZENSHIP NEED TO BE SHARED AND EXTENDED

Like Americans, the Romans thought of themselves as a nation of immigrants. The story of Rome's founding begins with Aeneas, a refugee from the burning city of Troy, who wanders the Mediterranean for years with his people searching for a new home, as told most poignantly in books two and three of Vergil's *Aeneid*. Romulus and Remus, Aeneas's descendants, actually founded the city of Rome as a new settlement and invited others to join them.[1] Despite these origin stories, the Romans could be ambivalent or even outright hostile to migrants. Yet they also did extend citizenship rights to non-Romans, that is, one did not have to be born a Roman; one could become a Roman, which comparatively speaking was a rather expansive view. Most ancient societies that had a concept of citizenship had a very strict understanding of who was a citizen. The Athenians, for all their reputed openness, typically did not permit non-citizens to become citizens; they allowed non-citizens to live with them, but these non-citizens, *metics* as they called them, were a separate class. The Romans, by contrast, had mechanisms for extending citizenship and citizen rights to non-Romans. This is not to say standards were always consistently applied or worked to the advantage of non-Romans. From time to time, the Romans expelled groups of people they found dangerous, including philosophers (161–154 BCE), Jews (139 BCE), Chaldeans (139 BCE), and worshippers of Bacchus (186 BCE).[2] The Romans could be undeniably brutal to conquered peoples, frequently killing and enslaving those they defeated in battle, but the Romans recognized that over time there were benefits to moving these defeated peoples from subjects to be governed to participants in the Roman political community.

As could be expected, the Romans gave citizenship, or a limited version of it, first to those who lived closest to them. Over time, the sense of who belonged to the Roman political community spread until in 212 CE the emperor Caracalla granted citizenship to all free peoples living within the boundaries of the Roman Empire.[3] However, as mentioned above, there were occasional complications to the process, and the Romans of the first century BCE faced the greatest citizenship crisis Rome ever had. For decades, Rome's Italian allies had been clamoring for some form of citizenship. Many Romans even recognized the legitimacy of their claim. After all, the Italian allies fought alongside Roman citizens in the army and frequently faced the greatest dangers. There was no denying that there would have been no Roman empire without the military service of the Italian allies, yet they were denied the greatest rewards of the empire.

As early as 125 BCE, proposals had been brought forth to grant the Italian allies Roman citizenship.[4] In 122 BCE, the tribune Gaius Gracchus, Tiberius's brother, tried to pass legislation to give some of Rome's allies the right to vote. His legislation failed, and in the controversy surrounding this proposal and others, violence broke out, resulting in his death. A generation later, in 91 BCE, the cause of Italian citizenship was taken up by another tribune, M. Livius Drusus, ironically the son of an opponent of Gaius Gracchus. Drusus had a broad legislative program, which sought to win support from all segments of society, but he nonetheless faced vigorous opposition from the senate. Despite his struggles to get his legislation passed, he persisted in pushing for Italian citizenship. While working to garner support for this initiative, he was assassinated in his home.[5] Advocating for Italian citizenship was risky business.

So why were proposals to extend citizenship to the Italians resisted? First, the Roman people, who had to vote to pass the law, resented the idea of their votes and rights being diluted by what would be a rather large increase in citizens; the Roman people narrow-mindedly wanted to maintain their privileges.[6] Second, the political elite resisted such proposals because they did not want any one individual to gain the credit, since the Roman politician who championed the legislation would receive a large base of Italian clients on whom he could rely for votes to further his political career. The inability of the Roman senate and people to solve this straightforward matter is the chief example of the Romans's incapacity and unwillingness to address problems with a spirit of serving the common good. Justice demanded that the Italian allies receive citizenship; moreover, it served the common defense of the country. The Romans collectively looked to their own private interests. The result was tragic.

Following decades of trying to use the Roman political system to gain citizenship, the Italians revolted upon the news of Livius Drusus's assassination. The Social War between Rome and its allies (*socii*) lasted for several years (91–88 BCE) and ended the way everyone could have predicted: thousands needlessly died, untold amounts of treasure were wasted, and the Italians were granted citizenship.[7] To be sure, the Romans won the war, after losing several battles, but it was unnecessary and revealed the political weakness of the Republic, which in the coming decades would struggle to solve the most basic questions confronting Rome. In addition, the Romans were fighting their allies at a time when they were being threatened by Mithridates, king of Pontus, who later in 88 BCE would massacre thousands of Romans and Italians in the province of Asia, over 80,000 in one day according to our sources.[8] The Romans were undoubtedly stronger militarily, politically, and socially with their Italian allies at their side. Their unwillingness to share political power cost them dearly and little seemed to be learned from the ordeal, though undoubtedly the war had the beneficial result of incorporating Italians into the Roman political system.

The United States has taken a long time to extend citizen rights beyond the limited number of citizens initially recognized in the Constitution.[9] The expansion of US citizenship and voting rights is a history of fits and starts: progress, resistance, and retrenchment followed by further advances. For example, women and Black Americans were sporadically given the right to vote, had it taken away, and then finally won the right against fierce opposition. Only after centuries has citizenship and voting rights expanded from White male landowners to include different races, genders, classes, nationalities and ethnicities, religions, and indigenous peoples. These rights have been hard-fought gains begrudgingly won, and their existence is tenuous. Although there is no such bill in any legislature in the United States seeking outright to strip Black Americans, for example, of their right to vote, one does not need to strip every Black American of their right to vote in order to win an election. Simply making it difficult for Black Americans to vote results in some not being able to vote, and often that is enough to win a close election. Following the 2020 presidential election, legislatures in Texas, Georgia, and Florida passed laws that tightened voting rights and access to the ballot.[10] The right to vote in the United States is an ongoing struggle.

Further, it is clear to any casual political observer that the United States is facing its own crisis over immigration and citizenship. Although the United States has been built and strengthened by immigrants, the question not only of who is allowed to be a citizen but also of who is simply allowed to enter the country has become fraught with peril. Such questions are endemic to the United States; nativism is a distinct part of American history. For decades, the immigration crisis has plagued the American political system, and for some of the same reasons as Rome, the United States has failed to productively address how to treat non-citizens.

Serious attempts to update our immigration policy go back several presidential administrations; all have failed to produce acceptable proposals. Just like for many Romans, many Americans resist immigration reform because they fear they will lose jobs or the power of their vote.[11] In addition, there is also opposition because some believe that former immigrants, now newly naturalized citizens, would form a voting block for the Democratic Party. Nonetheless, President Barack Obama earned the moniker "deporter in chief" from immigration advocates for the deportation of over two million people.[12] The failures of previous decades to address the Dreamers, Deferred Action for Childhood Arrivals (DACA) recipients, and migrants in general were exploited by the Trump administration which demonstrated the utmost hostility to migrants, particularly those coming from Latin America and the Middle East, even those seeking political asylum and serving in the military. Trump notoriously announced his candidacy for president in June 2015 by attacking Mexican immigrants, saying, "They're bringing drugs. They're bringing crime. They're rapists."[13] Trump's hostility toward immigrants extended even to those who serve in our military. Since 1940 foreign-born members of the armed services were able to submit an expedited application for citizenship. In 2017, the Trump administration, led by Stephen Miller, added further requirements making the process more burdensome for applicants. These additional requirements were challenged in court, and in August 2020, the new policy was overruled. Nonetheless, the episode demonstrates the efforts to tamp down on naturalized citizenship even for those risking their lives in defense of the United States.[14]

Even more disgracefully, the Trump administration proudly authorized the separation of children from their families and filled detention centers along the border and throughout the country. Americans were left to debate whether these were only holding facilities or internment camps, or even concentration camps.[15] Under the Trump presidency it was not an academic question to ask how many people needed to be detained and for how long before a detention center became an internment camp or concentration camp. Although a federal judge ordered families to be reunited, when Trump left office there were still between 600 and 1,000 families, parents and children, separated, many of whose whereabouts were unknown.[16] Although Trump repeatedly downplayed the seriousness of the coronavirus, he did not hesitate to use the pandemic to shut down the southern border, something he had long promised to do.[17]

Further, the more attacks against migrants are tolerated, the more US citizens, especially citizens of color, can be labeled as un-American and therefore subject to the same treatment as migrants. We have seen how the casual vilification of migrants has put US citizens of Latin American or Middle Eastern descent in danger. Davino Watson, a US citizen was held in detention by Immigration and Customs Enforcement (ICE) for over three years, 2008–11, during the Bush and Obama administrations. More recently, Francisco Galicia, an 18-year-old US citizen, was held by ICE for 23 days without a shower or adequate nutrition.[18] Trump even suggested the deportation of US citizens of color who had the audacity to question his political opinions, most prominently Rep. Ilhan Omar. Trump's attacks on US Representatives of color, saying they should "go back" to the "places from which they came," and his followers' chants of "send her back," were just the next logical step after separating children from their parents at the border and locking them up.[19] Mistreatment of migrants jeopardizes the safety of US citizens.

How will this end? Recent US immigration policy flies in the face of the evidence on immigration, which well records the great benefit immigrants from all lands have contributed to the success and prosperity of the United States.[20] The United States is wasting precious time and resources and creating untold suffering for thousands of lives. As late as January 12, 2021, Trump was visiting South Texas and falsely claiming, "We've completed the wall." A little over a week later, President Biden issued an executive order halting work on the wall, which was still incomplete.[21] Although President Biden seems to want to reform immigration policy, much of this may be limited to executive orders.[22] Moreover, even Biden has been reluctant to increase refugee admissions, and only increased them after intense pressure from his own party.[23] Given the inability and unwillingness to advance and support common sense immigration reform, it seems that the United States too, rather than seeking a humane and just solution aimed at the common good, is choosing an inconsistent path that will likely have tragic consequences for both migrants and American citizens.

Chapter 8

CIVIC VIRTUE IS AS IMPORTANT AS THE CONSTITUTION AND LAWS

If freedom and institutions are no bulwark against economic inequality, political violence, and the abuse of power, what remains? There remains the civic virtue of the citizens who are willing to defend the common good over personal advantage, that is, the practice of political forbearance and the willingness to resist the lure of undue private financial gain, violence against fellow citizens, and excessive political power. By the Late Republic, the Romans had built up a strong tradition of civic virtue. Many of the stories the Romans told about themselves were meant to provide examples of civic virtue, and although many of these stories were from the dim past or overly romanticized, they instructed generations of Romans to put the public good over private gain.

No story exemplified this better than the account of the dictatorship of Cincinnatus in 458 BCE. First, it should be noted that the Romans had a constitutional office of dictator that they would turn to in times of emergency, usually after a foreign army soundly defeated a Roman army. The dictator, as we might suspect, had broad powers; the Romans therefore put as many constraints on the dictator as possible while also giving him wide latitude to accomplish the necessary task. Therefore, the senate had to issue a decree authorizing the consuls to nominate a dictator, who was often then recognized formally by an assembly of the people, thereby giving consent to the broad powers. In addition, the dictator had a deputy, the master of horse, who was not necessarily the dictator's political ally. Lastly, the dictator was given six months to address the emergency; if he had not done so within that time, his office was up and other means were taken. We might imagine that an unscrupulous dictator could hold onto his power and use it to become master of the Roman people. The Romans were aware of this possibility too, but for over four hundred years, no dictator ever abused his power in this way, at least for long.[1]

In 458 BCE, the Sabines and Aequi had defeated Roman armies in the field, and there was need for a reliable commander. The current consul was deemed unfit for the task at hand, but Cincinnatus, now in retirement, had been an accomplished politician and general. As the story goes, he was cultivating his fields across the Tiber River, when the embassy of senators approached him.[2] The senators told him to put on his toga, the formal dress of a Roman as a citizen. With some concern, Cincinnatus complied with the request, whereupon the senators hailed him as dictator and escorted him across the Tiber. The senate had chosen wisely, for Cincinnatus put down the enemy threat and turned over his authority in 15 days, though he had six months. He could have reasonably and constitutionally held onto his command for another five months fabricating pretexts to justify his continued authority. Instead, he handed over the fasces, the Roman symbols of legitimate political and military power, and retired to his farm. For the Romans, several things were important about this story. First, service to the Republic took precedence over private gain—when one is called to serve the Republic, one puts aside one's personal work. Second, the public good prevailed over individual power—when the crisis is resolved, political power is handed over willingly. Lastly, Livy stresses that the story of Cincinnatus demonstrated the value of honor and courage over wealth.[3] Cincinnatus served as a reminder to the Romans that they should pursue the common virtues of hard work and civic responsibility, shunning luxury and personal wealth and power.

Lucius Cornelius Sulla provided another example—the individual who would use whatever means were available to hold onto power and violently crush his political enemies. In 83 BCE, Sulla returned to Italy fresh off his victory against Mithridates, not simply to parade in triumph and lay down his weapons, but to march on Rome once again and punish his enemies and reward his friends.[4] There were several bloody battles, after which Sulla slaughtered his defeated opponents. The bloodshed continued once formal military engagements ended. Sulla drew up proscription lists of his enemies numbering several thousand. Once Sulla had crushed his rivals, a leading senator proposed to make Sulla dictator for rewriting the laws and restructuring the constitution—a radical reshaping of the traditional office of dictator; the people, no doubt in terror, passed the proposal into law, thus giving Sulla constitutional legitimacy for his dictatorship.[5]

Unlike Cincinnatus, Sulla faced no immediate external threat to Rome; in fact, he had just defeated Rome's greatest external threat—Mithridates. Further there was no time limit to Sulla's authority as dictator. Sulla's reforms of the laws were not entirely harmful; some might have even been needed, such as those pertaining to membership in the senate, provincial government, and the law courts. However, he took a harsh view of the tribunes and popular measures; he abolished the distribution of grain to the poor and limited the power of the tribunes by restricting the use of their veto, removing their right to propose legislation, and making them ineligible for future offices. Sulla claimed to be a lawgiver and restorer of the traditional constitution, but he was lacking in civic virtue. His reforms served the aristocratic elite most of all, and he took violent means to achieve them.[6] His reform of the tribunate, which was contrary to tradition, would not stand for more than a decade and led to much animosity and civil strife. Sulla would not live to see much of this strife, as he retired from the dictatorship after two years (81–79 BCE) and died a year later. Several decades later, Caesar would declare himself dictator for life. The evil that Sulla had done and the precedents he had set lived after him.

The memory of Cincinnatus and Sulla would live on in the American psyche as well, at least for the Founders, who venerated Cincinnatus as a model of self-restraint. George Washington, upon leaving the presidency, was hailed as a second Cincinnatus.[7] Indeed, statues of Washington standing before a plow can be found at Mt. Vernon and the Virginia statehouse, symbolizing his return to a civilian's private life, though to be sure this is an idealized and nostalgic view—unlike Cincinnatus, who had his own hand on his plow when the senators arrived, Washington enslaved others to do his plowing for him. The city of Cincinnati carries on the legacy of Cincinnatus and boasts several public monuments to him. The idea of a public figure willingly surrendering power is an honored tradition and is publicly celebrated every time the newly elected president escorts the former president from the steps of the Capitol following the inauguration.

US citizens can no longer take this tradition for granted. Aside from refusing to attend President Biden's inauguration, Donald Trump and his followers came dangerously close to pulling off a successful coup on January 6, 2021, an insurrection that should have surprised no one as it was signaled well in advance. On December 19, 2020, Trump had tweeted of January 6, "Be there, will be wild!"[8] To understand how close Trump and his followers came to violently overturning a free and fair election, we must examine three crucial moments in the events that day.

The first moment came at the rally Trump held at the Ellipse. Although his rally was thoroughly predictable, it was also an utterly unprecedented event. Trump, a lame-duck president, held a rally challenging the election concurrently with the formal counting of state electoral ballots. Trump and his supporters repeated the lie that the election was stolen, that a vague cabal of forces had conspired to rob Trump of a second term. Trump inflamed his followers to a show of force by marching on the Capitol, urging them, "You'll never take back our country with weakness."[9] Just as Sulla was the first to march an army on Rome, so Trump was the first to incite his followers to attack the Capitol in an attempt to violently overturn a legitimate presidential election. Academics have quibbled over terms, but when political leaders rouse their followers to march with force against a nation's lawfully assembled representatives, particularly when those representatives are meeting to certify the election of a new leader, there is but one way to describe this act—it is an attempted coup.[10] Among the differences between Trump's most ardent followers and the majority of the American public is that his followers have taken him consistently at his word. They did not need convincing; they did not wait to parse the precise meaning of his words. They commenced to march on the Capitol to disrupt the certification of the presidential election.

The second crucial moment came when these marchers reached the steps of the Capitol and forced their way into the halls of Congress. The predominantly white crowd was met with faint resistance as they pushed their way through the doors. Protests for racial justice in 2020, against the Iraq War in 2003, and, to go even further back, the World Trade Organization (WTO) protests in Seattle in 1999, bear witness to the aggression and violence American security forces can muster. Yet a belligerent mob was able to break into the Capitol with faint resistance during the vote for certifying the 2020 presidential election. Almost entirely absent were tear gas canisters, armored vehicles, and flash bangs, to say nothing of guns and rubber bullets. White privilege nearly allowed these rioters to overturn a US presidential election. When the rioters reached the House floor, it was mere luck that legislators had escaped and House staffers had thought to take the boxes containing the electoral votes with them. Trump's followers came dangerously close to stealing and destroying the actual electoral ballots. Undoubtedly, such ballots could be resubmitted, but legitimacy accompanied the possessor of the actual, submitted ballots. With these electoral ballots destroyed or held hostage, Trump's supporters would have come remarkably close to achieving their objective, at least for a short time.[11] Further, these rioters were left to freely vacate the premises once they could not find what they had come to take; hardly an arrest was made on the premises.

The third and final moment came after the rioters left or were at last subdued and Congress was called back into session. There was much that was admirable in the determination with which the elected representatives and senators carried out the duty of counting the electoral votes. Indeed, witnessing congressional staffers carrying the boxes of electoral ballots back into the House of Representatives followed by the vice president was a moving scene for many, a scene of legitimate authority carrying out the will of the people. There were a number of inspiring and sobering speeches, particularly Senator Romney's, in part because the customary pretense that accompanies so much public speech had been stripped away. And yet, 147 legislators still found the temerity to argue for nullifying the votes of the people and their electors.[12] When Trump's followers entered the Capitol, they searched in vain for senators and representatives. If they had arrived just a bit sooner and had taken them hostage in the house and senate chambers, they would have found over 140 legislators sympathetic to their cause. Those representatives who persisted in objecting to the duly certified electoral ballots were engaged in the same pursuit as those who had scaled the walls of the Capitol, and that objective was to overturn the will and the votes of a majority of the American people.[13] At the time, many Republican lawmakers expressed outrage and a willingness to break from Trump, but in the months since Republican support for an independent commission on January 6 waned.[14] Trump and his access to campaign dollars have reasserted control over the GOP. Republicans have also cooled in their support because they now know what they did not as they were frantically barricading the doors to the House chamber on January 6— the angry mob was not coming for them; the mob was coming for House Speaker Nancy Pelosi, Representative Alexandria Ocasio-Cortez, and yes Vice President Mike Pence.[15]

Successful coups need two things—an effective show of force and a veneer of formality to supply legitimacy to what violence has achieved. January 6 had both of these elements. The only thing that prevented them from coming together to form a successful coup was timing. That rioters were kept at arm's length just long enough from the elected officials they were seeking was certainly the result of heroism from people like Officer Eugene Goodman, but it was also more accident than design.[16]

Donald Trump told his followers via Twitter, "Remember this day forever."[17] No doubt, they will. Although Trump's extremist followers failed in preventing the certification of the election, they succeeded beyond all expectation in breaching the walls of our Capitol. Moreover, neither Trump nor his congressional supporters have been held to account for their action. In fact, the opposite has occurred. Trump was acquitted in his second impeachment trial. The legislators who refused to accept the elections results even after the insurrection have experienced few repercussions, while many of those Republicans who voted for Trump's impeachment have been censured by their state Republican Party.[18] Moreover, Congressional Republicans have purged bona fide conservatives like Rep. Liz Cheney from leadership positions.[19] Rioters were able to enter the Capitol, murder, destroy property, and then exit largely without harm; some were arrested and charged, but most were left to go as they pleased.[20] Some commentators have mocked Rep. Andrew S. Clyde's statement that the rioters where merely on a "normal tourist visit"; yet given how many of them were treated, able to come and go at will, Rep. Clyde provides a somewhat apt description of what happened.[21]

What Sulla had but Trump lacked was a large, well-trained military force. In the end, Trump was no Sulla. US citizens would be foolish to give anyone the opportunity to become one. The comparison between Cincinnatus, Sulla, and Trump, however, is not simply about military might and what it can accomplish. The point really is about the exercise of political forbearance, or the lack thereof, in the service of civic virtue. Cincinnatus surrendered his political power early and willingly. Sulla and Trump abused their authority in an attempt to stay in office beyond their term and were willing to use violence to do so. Sulla's dictatorship hastened the fall of the Roman Republic. Americans would be wise not to underestimate the nature of what happened on January 6. It was unprecedented and it was an attempted coup.

Chapter 9

A RECKONING WITH THE OPPRESSED CANNOT BE DENIED

The brutality between Romans witnessed in the Sullan civil wars and proscriptions was matched by the daily violence visited upon the enslaved. From time to time, the Roman Republic experienced uprisings by those seeking liberation from the system that kept them in bondage. The enslaved conducted several significant revolts in Sicily, a hotbed of resistance. In 135 BCE, led by Eunus and Cleon, over 70,000 enslaved people revolted and trained themselves into a formidable fighting force; it took several years and several consular armies to subdue them. In 104 BCE, uprisings occurred at Capua in Italy and again in Sicily led by Salvius and Athenion, who successfully held off Roman armies until 101 BCE.[1] As serious as these earlier uprisings were, the most significant revolt of the Late Republic happened in 73–71 BCE under the leadership of Spartacus.

A few brief words are needed regarding Roman slavery.[2] First and foremost, Americans need to know that Roman slavery was not based on race or skin color as is commonly assumed. Roman slavery was an economic system that did not rely on an ideology such as race to sustain it. Indeed, Romans were not enslaved by other Romans, and the Romans did think they were superior to the enslaved, but skin color had nothing to do with who ended up enslaved in ancient Rome, and it should be pointed out that many White Northern Europeans would have been found among the enslaved in Rome.[3] The most common ways to become enslaved in Roman society were either to be born to a parent who was enslaved or to be captured in war or piracy, which suggests there was an element of fortune, not simply nature, bound up in it.[4] *Servus*, the most common Latin word for an enslaved person, is thought to refer to those pre*served* from war, that is, those left alive after the battle. Thus, the enslaved could be from Greece, Spain, Northern and Central Europe, North and Sub-Saharan Africa, and the Middle East, if not even further afield.

The enslaved in Roman society worked a whole range of activities from being language tutors to digging in the mines. Nearly any work that could be done the enslaved did. Some of the enslaved might have had a decent standard of living, such as Tiro, who served as Cicero's secretary until he was manumitted, a common feature of Roman life, but many lived insufferable lives; all of them were denied liberty. The oppression of Roman slavery was grinding as all slavery is. Tacitus provides a representative story. In 61 CE under the reign of Nero, Pedanius Secundus was killed by one of the people he enslaved over a disagreement. Roman law required all those enslaved in the household, over four hundred, to be executed along with the person who carried out the actual murder; this law had recently been made harsher to include even those who had been manumitted. The common people of Rome protested this act of excessive cruelty and initially succeeded in holding off the executions, but the senate and the emperor Nero persisted in carrying out the executions.[5] Given such brutal treatment, it should be unsurprising that resistance against this oppression was not an uncommon facet of Roman society.

Spartacus was a Thracian enslaved as a gladiator in Capua.[6] He and his comrades had had enough of the cruel mistreatment from their overseers and used their training to escape. They met with surprising success and properly armed themselves with the weapons confiscated from the Roman armies they defeated. As Spartacus and his army roamed the countryside, they liberated the enslaved and grew into a formidable military force, defeating even a consular army. The Romans as often underestimated the level of resistance and sophistication of their opponents, and Spartacus and his allies overcame numerous Roman armies as he marched throughout Italy looking for a way to escape, first over the Alps, then with Cilician pirates, and lastly to Sicily.

In the end, the Romans brutally crushed Spartacus and his supporters. Following the defeats suffered by several Roman commanders, Marcus Licinius Crassus was given the command and six legions in 72 BCE. Crassus first punished his own Roman soldiers who had deserted in the face of Spartacus's army by reviving the practice of decimation, the execution of one out of every ten men in a selected group of soldiers. This brutality presaged the violent treatment of the survivors of Spartacus's revolt. In the spring of 71 BCE, Crassus managed to corral Spartacus in southern Italy and forced him into a decisive battle. Though Spartacus's body was never found, the defeat of his forces effectively ended the revolt. As a sign to all, free and enslaved, the Romans crucified 6,000 captives along the Appian Way, Rome's major thoroughfare across Italy from Rome to Brundisium. Crucifixion was the form of capital punishment used for non-Romans and was commonly applied. The Romans used force to put down resistance to slavery; they never confronted the institution of slavery, and very few individuals from antiquity, including Christians, questioned its legitimacy.[7] For the Romans, the answer to challenges to violent oppression was more oppression and violence.

In fact, very few people questioned the legitimacy of slavery until the nineteenth century, and slavery, though illegal, still exists as you are reading this in the form of human trafficking, as mentioned in the Introduction. The United States abolished slavery in 1865 through the Thirteenth Amendment, with the exception of those who have been convicted of a crime.[8] Yet slavery has had a lasting effect on American life not only because of its economic impact but most profoundly because of the element of racism bound up with it; the connection between American slavery and racism has allowed the inequities of slavery to persist and fester. Slavery gave way to Jim Crow, and Jim Crow has given way to mass incarceration, which is compounded by police brutality against Black Americans.[9] Slavery and race have deeply affected nearly every aspect of American life from where we live, work and worship to our wealth, well-being, and education.

There is much more to say about slavery and racism in America than space here allows, but its lasting impact in large part can be traced to the failure to provide reparations to the newly freed and formerly enslaved.[10] This failure to reckon with slavery and its attendant racism has scarred American civic life. In many ways, America is a young democracy. The claims to democracy, freedom, and equality that are enshrined in our founding documents were never realized until 1965 following the passage of the Civil Rights Act of 1964 and the Voting Rights Act of 1965. Even still, the structures of racism and white supremacy remain with us. The health disparities that have always existed in America between Blacks and Whites have been on full display during the pandemic, which has disproportionately afflicted communities of color.[11] Further, the backlash to America's first Black president has been swift and strong, propelling Donald Trump to the White House. Trump's campaign and presidency were nourished by white grievance and were accompanied by the rise and proliferation of white supremacist groups. The assault against the Capitol on January 6 was a demonstration of white supremacy as much as anything. As Rev. Bryan Massingale has so eloquently stated, the assault on the Capitol was "a clear declaration that many white people would rather live in a white dictatorship than in a multiracial democracy."[12] The unwillingness of Trump and his followers to accept the results of a fair and free election was nothing less than the attempt to disenfranchise millions of voters of color, the majority of whom voted for Joe Biden.

Societies like ancient Rome or modern America can continue their oppression of millions of people and still "prosper." Rome used great violence to maintain its system of enslavement and the wealth it created for its elites. For centuries, the United States has used terror and violence to oppress Black people, from which its White citizens have profited greatly; the wealth disparity between Blacks and Whites demonstrates this clearly.[13] The United States will have to face this, willingly or unwillingly. Will we continue to be a country that serves white privilege at the cost of terrorizing and oppressing millions of its citizens or will the United States commit to becoming a fully formed democratic republic at last? This is not an abstract question and it is not a question that will quietly go away for the United States despite the wishes of many of its citizens. It will have to be answered. As the Roman imperial philosopher Seneca wrote, "Fate leads the willing, the unwilling it drags."[14]

Chapter 10

ELECTIONS ONLY WORK WHEN EVERYONE IS WILLING TO LOSE

Despite Sulla's dictatorship, Roman elections continued for the most part as they had for the previous four centuries. Further, the powers he stripped from the tribunes were restored over the next decade. These developments were a welcome return to the traditions of the Roman constitution, but in many ways, they were a return to normalcy in appearance only. For in many ways, the Roman electoral system was in crisis. First, from the time of Tiberius Gracchus, violence had become a regular part of Roman assemblies, as noted earlier. Second, bribery and corruption had become a common feature of Roman elections. The Romans did attempt to address the issue of bribery and passed any number of laws to restrict it. One such law was passed in 67 BCE, which was immediately put to use in the consular elections for 66 BCE; the two candidates who received the most votes were prosecuted for bribery and were prevented from taking office. This law and its effective enforcement is one example of the Romans's attempt to respond to their political crises.

The third challenge Roman elections had to confront was a result of the first two, namely legitimacy and a subsequent unwillingness to abide peacefully by the election results. In the consular election of 63 BCE, among the candidates was Lucius Sergius Catiline. Catiline had made a fortune in the Sullan proscriptions, which he subsequently squandered, and he personally took part in the brutal murder and mutilation of Marcus Marius Gratidianus, nephew of Gaius Marius.[1] Catiline had run in 64 BCE for consul, but lost to Gaius Antonius and Cicero. The threat of violence loomed over the consular elections in 63 BCE; they even had to be postponed once. As an indication of the dangers he faced presiding over the election, Cicero conspicuously wore a breastplate into the Campus Martius where the elections were held.[2] To the relief of many Romans, Catiline lost again in 63 BCE despite making radical promises to cancel all debts and engaging in extensive bribery, both symptoms of economic inequality. But Catiline, unable to secure another political office from which he could pay off his debts, was a desperate man willing to take desperate measures. Catiline allied with some of Sulla's veterans, who, no longer having a patron to call upon, were aggrieved at having fallen into debt, and together they conspired to overthrow the Roman government. This plot has become known to history as the Catilinarian Conspiracy. Following a strong speech in the senate from the consul Cicero accusing Catiline, he left Rome and joined up with the forces gathering in the countryside, where they had been stockpiling weapons.[3] Some of Catiline's partisans remained in Rome, but they were foiled by Cicero and their plot to light fire to the city was revealed. Among the conspirators was Publius Autronius Paetus, one of the consular candidates convicted of bribery in 66 BCE. Cicero dispatched his consular colleague, Gaius Antonius, to Etruria where he fought and defeated Catiline in battle early in 62 BCE. Cicero was escorted home as a hero the night Catiline's partisans in the city were executed; Marcus Porcius Cato, frequently called Cato the Younger, hailed him as *pater patriae*—"father of the fatherland," an honorific rarely invoked.[4]

It is too easy to vilify Catiline, not least of all for his moral shortcomings. Catiline was symptomatic of a corrupt political environment. Nonetheless, Catiline and his co-conspirators demonstrated exactly what was at stake in Roman elections. Moreover, he revealed the capacity for unscrupulous demagogues to feed off the economic desperation of the lower classes. Lastly, the conspiracy raised the ongoing concern that the results of the next election would not be respected. It could no longer be assumed that the candidates and the people would abide by the results of an election, whether they based their arguments for illegitimacy on bribery, violence, or economic anxiety. In the case of Catiline, all three were at work.

American elections had fallen into a crisis of legitimacy well before the 2020 presidential election and Trump's January 6 coup attempt. Shameless partisanship has gerrymandered the electoral map, ensuring victories for a party that should be in the minority and requiring supermajorities to gain victory for a party that should be in the majority; by no definition is this democracy. The 2000 election was marred by turmoil and recounts in Florida. In addition, the elections in 2000 and 2016 have brought results in which the popular vote and the Electoral College vote were at odds. Although the Electoral College is an undeniable, even if controversial, feature of the US Constitution, most Americans view such imbalanced results as undemocratic, and it is hard to argue otherwise. In fact, the intention behind the creation of the Electoral College was undemocratic and an example of how the Founders sought to detach higher offices from the direct vote of the people. They took a somewhat similar approach with US Senators, who were originally elected by state legislatures. Although many Americans have come to consider many aspects of the original Constitution, which the Founders deemed acceptable, now to be undemocratic or out of date and have subsequently amended the document, nonetheless, the Electoral College persists.

Beyond these sources of distrust, there are even newer challenges to the electoral system in the United States. Foremost among them is the manipulation of US elections from outsiders, specifically the Russians, who have demonstrably tampered with US elections and have engaged in electronic campaigns of disinformation. This was at work in the 2016 presidential election and is ongoing, as Special Counsel Robert Mueller warned Congress in the summer of 2019, "They are doing it as we sit here."[5]

Outside interference, however, was hardly needed to threaten the electoral process. Well before the 2020 presidential election, Donald Trump cast seeds of doubt on its validity and threatened violence if he was not elected just as he did before the 2016 election; he even proposed postponing the 2020 election.[6] As a candidate in 2016, when pondering with his constituents that nothing could be done if Hillary Clinton won the presidency, he said, "Although the Second Amendment people—maybe there is, I don't know."[7] He threatened violence similarly before the Republican National Convention in 2016, warning if he were not nominated, "I think you'd have riots."[8] Even after winning the 2016 election, Trump continued to cast doubt over the legitimacy of the popular vote, which favored Hillary Clinton. In both the 2016 and 2020 elections, Trump was repeatedly asked if he would abide by the result of the election. Trump equivocated whether he would, but in a world where the question even needs to be asked, there can be no doubt that some, including Trump himself, considered that they would not accept the election results. The civic virtue of the president should not be in question.

It was not hard to foresee a man of Trump's temperament refusing to yield the White House following an election that he and others deemed illegitimate. Despite the president being constitutionally limited to two terms, Trump repeatedly hinted that he could stay in office beyond that time; his initial tweet after his first impeachment acquittal showed a mock-up of a *Time* magazine cover of Trump campaign yard signs with dates stretching into the future.[9] Of course, he maintained plausible deniability, claiming that he was just trying to rile up the media, but this was just another way to test the waters of public opinion, which is why he and anyone must be challenged every time such autocratic designs are suggested. Yet it was not just the president saying this. Following the Democratic presidential debate on June 26, 2019, longtime Senator Lindsey Graham even tweeted, "that whole Trump 3rd term thing is looking better and better."[10] Of course, this was all before the election for Trump's *second* term. Graham's words were not just rhetoric; following Joe Biden's victory in Georgia, Senator Graham would actively interfere in the recount and certification of the vote.[11] Such loyalty from an ardent supporter of the president would not be so shocking if it were not coming from a senator whose constitutionally mandated job is in part to be a check on the power of the presidency. Some may assert with confidence that the Constitution prevents the president from holding a third term, as is indeed true, but Trump himself claimed that he was not limited by the Constitution. In a speech before the Turning Point USA Student Summit in Washington, DC, on July 23, 2019, he said of the Constitution, "I have an Article II, where I have the right to do whatever I want as president." During his impeachment trial, Trump's defense team repeatedly argued that the president was above the law; Alan Dershowitz went so far as to say "If a president does something which he believes will help him get elected in the public interest, that cannot be the kind of quid pro quo that results in impeachment." Undaunted by impeachment, Trump continued to view the pandemic as an opportunity to expand his authority, declaring at an April 13, 2020 news conference, "when somebody is the president of the United States, the authority is total, and that's the way it's going to be."[12]

Given all the statements by Trump and his supporters before the 2020 election, Trump's behavior following the 2020 presidential election should not have been surprising. Trump repeatedly pressured elected state officials to overturn certified election results, most shamelessly in Georgia where Trump called the Republican Secretary of State Brad Raffensperger on several occasions asking him to find the necessary votes to give him the victory.[13] The presidential election of 2020 was not a close election. Without the efforts of Trump to overturn the election, analysis of the results would have focused on Biden's impressive victories in Georgia and Arizona or on the record turnout. Instead, the nation was subjected to over two months of assault on our democratic process, culminating in the attempted coup of January 6.[14] Six months after the election, the Arizona State Senate ordered a review of the Maricopa County vote under highly questionable guidelines. In May 2021, a state judge in Georgia ordered that local voters could inspect all mail-in ballots from Fulton County for the 2020 presidential election.[15] There is no indication that contesting an election is a phenomenon limited to 2016 and 2020 or to Republican candidates; in fact, it seems more likely that the 2022 and 2024 elections will look a lot like the 2020 election, and both sides can replicate the tactics Trump has introduced into the electoral process.

The US electoral system has corruption, distrust, and manipulation. The only aspect from the Roman crisis lacking had been violence. The assault on the Capitol January 6 changed that.[16] The American people face not only the question of which candidates they will elect, but also how and whether they will prevent violence from infiltrating elections. Although violence has been largely absent from polling places and the campaign trail, there is little to prevent this from happening in the next election.

Chapter 11

DISREGARD FOR THE CIVIL LIBERTIES OF SOME ERODES THE LEGAL RIGHTS OF ALL CITIZENS

The Catilinarian Conspiracy did more than show the violence that can arise when citizens are not willing to accept the results of an election. Violence itself is often employed by the state in its response to the threat of conspiracy, or simply, perceived conspiracy. Undoubtedly, Catiline was up to something suspicious; the fact that he was defeated at the head of an army hostile to the Roman government suggests that his designs presented a serious threat to Rome. However, the legal handling of his co-conspirators who were captured in Rome before they could meet up with Catiline raised basic questions about Roman justice. A fundamental aspect of Roman law, which has been long admired, was the idea that a Roman accused of a crime was entitled to a trial. During the Catilinarian Conspiracy, however, the Roman senate had passed a Final Decree, just as it had against Gaius Gracchus and Saturninus, permitting Cicero, as consul, to execute the conspirators captured in Rome without a trial.

In the senate meeting that debated the fate of the conspirators, famously recorded by Sallust, the senate favored executing the conspirators until Julius Caesar rose to speak.[1] Caesar opposed execution, and as Rome had no prison system, he argued for the milder sentence of spreading the conspirators around Italy in virtual house arrest. Caesar was convincing, basing his argument on the Roman disinclination to put Roman citizens to death, certainly not without a trial. Caesar was opposed on this occasion, as on so many others, by Cato. Cato spoke persuasively in favor of executing the conspirators, arguing that the conspirators were now enemies of Rome, the city was still under threat, and the defense of the Republic was the greatest good. Although Cato won the day and the senate voted for execution, the Catilinarian Conspiracy was not Cato's finest hour. Cato would go on to be an outspoken critic of Caesar's authoritarianism and aberrations from the Roman constitution; he defended institutions and the rule of law at a time when few were willing to do so.

However, his eagerness to oppose Caesar and his harshness toward fellow Roman citizens put him on the wrong side of history this time.

The senate could not pass laws; it could only advise a presiding magistrate, which in this case was Cicero. This actually gave quite a bit of cover to Cato and other senators who were in favor of execution. It put the full responsibility on Cicero, who took the senate's decree as having the force of law. He acted to have the conspirators executed immediately; for Cicero, who otherwise did as much as any Roman to save the Republic, executing the conspirators extrajudicially was an unfortunate move. At the time, emotions were overheated and people were in fear. Regret, however, began to set in quickly after the execution of the conspirators, as Cicero was not allowed to give the customary account of his year in office, and in the years following, a backlash against Cicero grew.[2] In 58 BCE, his nemesis Publius Clodius Pulcher, as tribune, passed a law exiling anyone who had put a Roman citizen to death without a trial; it was clear to all that Cicero was the target. Cicero, hailed as the father of the country in the aftermath of the conspiracy, was forced into exile in March of 58 BCE, until public sentiment once again turned and the assembly, under Gnaeus Pompey's direction, voted for Cicero's recall in August 57 BCE.[3] Nonetheless, the execution of fellow Romans without a trial would remain a mark against Cicero's otherwise positive record of public service and raised lingering questions about the Roman legal system.

At the US presidential inauguration, the incoming president swears to oppose all enemies, foreign and domestic. The question of domestic enemies has taken on a new weight in the aftermath of September 11, 2001, when laws were hastily passed, most notably the USA PATRIOT Act, to gird up America's defenses against terrorism and to calm an anxious citizenry. These laws were in addition to America's already harsh laws on drugs and immigration. Although the most troubling aspects of these anti-terrorism laws were pointed out, assurances were made that they would not be turned against peaceful US citizens—not the highest standard of justification when it comes to human rights.[4] Over the decades, we have seen how such laws against terrorism have been used against US citizens abroad, as in the assassination of US citizens Anwar al-Awlaki (in Yemen under President Obama), his 16-year-old son Abdulrahman (in a separate attack in Yemen under President Obama), and his 8-year-old daughter Nawar (in still another separate attack in Yemen under President Trump).[5] Arguments, however flimsy, have been made to justify such deaths. The concern about taking such a cavalier approach to the application of US law is that it elides the distinctions between citizens/non-citizens, permanent residents/migrants, combatants/non-combatants. US citizens domestically who are seen in the eyes of the administration as enemies or threats of the state can easily be harassed. Just as the attack against immigrants provides space for White nationalists to recategorize citizens of color as immigrants, so the laws against terrorism allow the administration to categorize domestic groups as terrorists.

As the attack on the Capitol makes clear, the United States does face domestic terrorism threats, but frequently concerns of what constitutes a threat are misdirected. For example, Senators Ted Cruz and Bill Cassidy attempted to label antifa, a highly decentralized movement, a terrorist organization; Trump echoed their call.[6] Although antifa protestors have been controversial and have shown themselves willing to respond to White nationalist violence with force of their own, no one has died at their hands. Antifa has little organizational structure and has not enacted violence against the US government, all of which is in direct contrast to White nationalists, whom the Congress and Trump have been reluctant to confront or even disavow. In fact, Trump was willing to create a false equivalency between the violent actions of White nationalists in El Paso and Charlottesville and those who have stood against such violence. Just days after a White supremacist killed 22 people in the anti-immigrant attack in El Paso, the president was willing to equate such actions with antifa, claiming he was against hate groups, "Whether it's white supremacy, whether it's any other kind of supremacy. Whether it's antifa."[7] Trump's false equivalency implies that whatever actions are taken against White supremacy should also be taken against antifa. The militarized response to Black Lives Matter protests compared to the feeble response to the storming of the Capitol on January 6 is a stark reminder of the unequal treatment of US citizens, despite the growing evidence that White supremacist groups pose the gravest domestic security threat.[8]

The idea that tyrants target their own citizens as a hostile enemy goes back to antiquity and Aristotle.[9] The fact that US politicians are blithely willing to label some US citizens terrorists, while overlooking those who are an actual threat, should give all citizens pause, just as all citizens should be appalled by the Obama and Trump administrations's assassinations of US children. When due legal process is denied to migrants and US citizens are labeled enemy combatants or terrorists, no matter their age or actual threat, the due process rights of all US citizens are threatened.[10]

Chapter 12

MILITARY MISADVENTURES ABROAD LEAD TO INSTABILITY AT HOME

The Romans did not lose wars. In fact, the Middle and Late Republic are periods of almost continuous Roman success; yes, they lost battles, but they nearly always won the war. Despite this success, military campaigns still had the potential to be disruptive to political life at home. The resources devoted to them and the political divisiveness they caused wore away notions of the common good, political solidarity, and social trust. Thus, Sulla and Marius viewed the war against Mithridates, who had orchestrated the murder of thousands of Romans and Italians, not only as the serious threat to Rome it was, but also as an opportunity for personal aggrandizement; the consequences of their ambition and violence were devastating for Rome and thousands of its citizens who died in the resulting strife. Later conflicts had similar impacts.

In 60 BCE, Rome's three most powerful, richest, and ambitious men, Pompey, Crassus, and Caesar, decided to form a political alliance, which historians call the First Triumvirate. Pompey was the most successful militarily and the richest. He had strung together a number of unprecedented offices and military commands throughout the 70s and 60s BCE. The first elected office he ever held was the consulship, a violation of Roman custom; he also held sweeping commands against the Mediterranean pirates and concluded the protracted war against Mithridates, expanding Rome's empire into the Eastern Mediterranean. The commands, which he executed efficiently and effectively, granted him immense power; his authority against the pirates troubled senators because he did not have a colleague in the office, an unrepublican precedent. His career would later serve as a model for Augustus, Rome's first emperor.[1]

Caesar's career was on the rise, and though he had been a successful military commander, he did not yet have a distinctive military achievement to rival Pompey; in addition, he was indebted to men like Crassus. Crassus, a wealthy slum lord, was infamous for his remark that a man was not rich unless he had the money to buy an army.[2] Though powerful and wealthy, he barely had any military success, save suppressing the revolt of Spartacus, from the Roman perspective hardly the stuff to win a proper triumph. Crassus and Caesar were zealous for military triumphs that would give them the same distinction as Pompey and the plunder that would come with it. One could argue that their military ambitions, and the accommodation of those ambitions, were the most direct cause of the Republic's demise. The extraordinary commands that were granted to Caesar and Crassus were a threat to Rome whether they succeeded, in the case of Caesar, or failed, in the case of Crassus.

After holding the consulship in 59 BCE, Caesar was assigned to govern the provinces of Cisalpine Gaul and Transalpine Gaul beginning in 58 BCE. Unlike most provincial appointments, which lasted a year or two, Caesar's appointment, which was granted by the people rather than the senate, was established for five years; he would have the command extended for another five years, an unprecedented scenario. Cato and others resisted this extraordinary appointment, but Pompey used force to stifle the opposition and carry the vote for Caesar.[3] Although this appointment was an administrative post like many held by provincial governors, everyone understood that Caesar's intention was to use the position to initiate a campaign against the Gauls across the Alps. Presently, Rome was under no direct threat from the Gallic peoples north of the Alps. Nonetheless, the Romans had fought some intense wars with the Gauls; they hated and distrusted them. Caesar exploited this feeling to orchestrate a justification, a *casus belli*, for invading Gaul. Caesar enjoyed great success, and the war became incredibly popular among Romans. Every year, Caesar sent back to Rome reports on the war. These elegantly written commentaries, which became known as the *Gallic Wars*, created a sense of nationalistic fervor for the war and shrewdly depicted Caesar as the ideal Roman commander—by all accounts, especially his own, he was quite capable.

Caesar's campaigns in Gaul, however, were problematic for several reasons. First, Caesar's *casus belli* was tenuous; to initiate hostilities, he took advantage of the migration of Gallic peoples as if it were an invasion, though it does not seem too many Romans were concerned with this pretext. Second, Caesar in essence undertook a genocide of the Gallic peoples. Hundreds of thousands, if not millions, of Gauls were killed in the course of the campaign, which violated several treaties. The only Roman who seemed to have any misgivings over Caesar's violence and disregard for treaties was Cato, who objected that Caesar had actually broken treaties in his conquests. Cato insisted that Caesar had broken the law and should return to Rome for trial.[4] Caesar's victories and the wealth they poured into Rome drowned out Cato's calls for justice. Cato also feared the power that Caesar was accruing: his soldiers became fiercely loyal to him and had gained immense experience in battle; he had heaped up great wealth; and his popularity in Rome was unsurpassed. All of this created the opportunity for Caesar to return to Rome as a would-be tyrant.

This was a few years in the future; for the present, Caesar was still checked by the money, power, and fame of Pompey and Crassus, who were jointly elected consuls in 55 BCE. In 54 BCE, Crassus left for the province of Syria to begin his campaign against the Parthians. After plundering the Temple in Jerusalem, Crassus advanced east into Mesopotamia.[5] The Parthians possessed a proud and formidable kingdom on Rome's eastern border, stretching from the Indus River in the east to the Euphrates in the west and from the Persian Gulf in the south to the Caspian Sea in the north with its capital located at Ecbatana, in modern day Iran. Crassus, however, did not succeed as Caesar did in Gaul. In fact, his failed campaign provided the exception to the rule of Roman military success. In 53 BCE, he was defeated and killed at Carrhae, one of Rome's worst losses ever. In his quest to become a new Alexander, Crassus unwittingly led his men into a massacre and lost several Roman standards, a grave disgrace. Only the spirited defense put up by Gaius Cassius Longinus, the future tyrannicide, prevented the Parthians from invading the Roman province of Syria. Of the roughly 40,000 soldiers Crassus took with him, only about 10,000 returned alive. Crassus himself was ignominiously killed; his head was cut off and used as a prop in a Parthian staged Greek tragedy. The results of Crassus's defeat were indeed tragic for Rome: the loss of 30,000 soldiers, the squandering of resources, and the elimination of a restraint to the ambitions of Pompey and Caesar, whom a later poet, Lucan, would describe respectively as being unable to tolerate an equal or to abide a superior.[6] Rome did not need to go to war in either Gaul or Parthia; these wars were undertaken solely for the vainglory of the generals. Rome's proud and capable military had been put in the service of strongmen, who primarily pursued their own ambitions, not the common good of Rome. The Republic was now in the position of being able to endure neither the victory nor the defeat of its military.

The US war in Iraq was founded on a lie—there were no weapons of mass destruction. The adage that truth is the first casualty of war held true. Like Caesar, the Bush administration manufactured a *casus belli*—weapons of mass destruction—wholly devoid of veracity. But it was not simply principles that have been sacrificed in the War on Terror.[7] America has avoided the military disaster Crassus met in the Middle East, but its loss of life and treasure has been no less dear. Brown University's Costs of War Project reported in 2020 the number of US deaths in the wars in Iraq, Afghanistan, and Pakistan, including service members and contractors, as over 14,000; the total number of dead since 2001 surpasses 800,000.[8] The economic cost has reached six trillion dollars. Although successive administrations promised to end these wars—President Bush declared the "mission accomplished" in Iraq on May 1, 2003—they continued on in the background of American political life for 20 years until the ignominious withdraw of US troops from Afghanistan in the summer of 2021. Events in Afghanistan since the US troop withdrawal are still unfolding, but the swift resurgence of the Taliban and their resumption of power demonstrate the limitations of American power abroad, leading many to question what was gained over America's 20-year occupation of the country.[9]

The funds spent on the War on Terror could have been put to use on nation building in the United States, which has seen the deterioration of its education system and infrastructure after decades of tax cuts and deferred maintenance, or on foreign aid that would build goodwill and improve the quality of life for many around the world. The lives of the wounded and their family members have been upended with little accomplished militarily to show for it. Americans have seen their civil liberties diminished and their privacy eroded. The relationship with our allies has been challenged and the United States's reputation on the world stage has been greatly weakened. The result, despite any victories, such as the deaths of Osama bin Laden or Saddam Hussein, is a United States that has greater economic inequality and political polarization at home and less authority in the world abroad. These circumstances put our republic at risk to genuine terror threats, domestically and abroad, and to hostile nations, such as Russia. Trump's pardon of convicted Blackwater guards in December 2020 reminded Americans and Iraqis of the enduring wounds caused by the war.[10] Yet nowhere was the reminder of America's enduring divisions, both foreign and domestic, made clearer than after January 6 when over 20,000 National Guard troops occupied Washington, DC, and declared around the Capitol a Green Zone, a term Americans had come to equate with the violent instability of Baghdad.[11] There was a sense that the war had come home.

Chapter 13

ORGANIZED, ARMED GANGS TEAR APART A POLITICAL SYSTEM

At the same time as Rome was experiencing victory and defeat abroad, it was becoming an increasingly violent society at home. Rome had been marred by political violence for decades, but something had inherently changed. Violence, rather than being a shocking aberration, had become the political process. It was normal. Moreover, it was not simply directed at or carried out by political elites and generals. Unlike the murder of Tiberius Gracchus by a senatorial mob or the civil war of Marius and Sulla with organized armies, Roman citizens were now clashing with Roman citizens in the streets of Rome.

Violence in Rome became prevalent through organized political gangs. The Roman people had long been members of various organizations called *collegia*. Some *collegia* were based on geography, some were for workers of certain guilds or trades, and others seem to have been simply social clubs; frequently they had a religious cult associated with them. As Rome became more volatile politically, many *collegia* became vehicles for organizing political gangs. For this reason they were all abolished in 64 BCE, save the most respectable and venerable, but in 58 BCE, the radical tribune Publius Clodius repealed the law of 64 BCE thereby allowing the *collegia* to operate as political gangs once more.[1] Of course, the revival of the *collegia* was self-serving legislation, since Clodius promptly organized *collegia* that he would use to intimidate voters, threaten political enemies, and rough up the opposition.

The opposition did not tolerate this for long. They had their own money and political connections that could be used to form political gangs of their own. Pompey, who had become an object of Clodius's venom, saw to the creation of a rival gang, led by Titus Annius Milo, who was as ruthless as Clodius even if of a different political persuasion. In the forum and assemblies, the rival gangs of Clodius and Milo would go at each other or target those suspected of aiding the other side.[2] Since Rome had no official police force, there was little that could be done to restrain these gangs once they had been legalized, short of bringing soldiers into the city to restore order, a prospect few wanted. The result was that for the better part of the 50s BCE, Rome would be at the mercy of violent political gangs.

The violence in 53 BCE was so bloody that it blocked the elections, and Rome entered 52 BCE without any elected officials, an *interregnum* as the Romans called it, an irregular period after the term of the previous year's magistrates had ended but without their replacements in office. The disruptions of the elections were in the shadow of Crassus's defeat at Carrhae and unrest in Caesar's Gaul. It was not a good time for Rome to be without its highest officeholders. By chance in January of 52 BCE, Clodius and Milo, accompanied by their gangs, met on the Appian Way, south of Rome. In the ensuing fight, Clodius received the worst of it and was wounded. His supporters took him to a nearby inn with Milo in pursuit; Milo's men dragged Clodius outside and killed him.[3]

When Clodius's dead body was brought back to Rome, the city erupted in rioting. Clodius's supporters took his body to the senate house in the forum and set the building ablaze to serve as Clodius's funeral pyre. The senate declared martial law and rather than wait any longer, the Romans did something that was contradictory to their constitution and practically unimaginable—in February 52 BCE, they elected one man to serve as consul, Gnaeus Pompey. This solution was at odds with Rome's traditional constitution and a harbinger of autocratic rule in the name of security. Presumably Romans felt uncomfortable electing a dictator following Sulla's violent abuse of power; yet rather than giving Pompey the dictator's six months, they gave him the ten months that were left of 52 BCE as sole consul. In the summer of 52 BCE, Pompey selected a colleague, his father-in-law Metellus Pius Scipio. He promptly passed several laws against electoral bribery and public violence. Milo, defended by Cicero, was put on trial; Clodius's rabid supporters threatened the proceedings, and Pompey was compelled to station troops in the forum. Milo was found guilty, as he surely was, and was forced to endure a comfortable exile in Massilia (Marseilles) for several years.[4] He would return to Italy in 48 BCE to foment a rebellion among the poor and was subsequently killed, an end Clodius would likely have found fitting.[5]

The violence of the political gangs profoundly impacted Rome. Ordinary Roman citizens were intimidated from participating in the political process, elections were delayed, a sole consul had been put into power, and martial law declared. This is to say little of those who suffered the direct effects of violent mobs. A republican society can endure such things for only so long.

Throughout its history, the United States has seen political violence and terrorism. The Ku Klux Klan is perhaps the best example of American citizens organizing to terrorize and dominate other citizens.[6] Vigilantes were also long active in anti-union efforts; the Pinkertons were the most notorious anti-union organization, but violence and intimidation were often ad hoc.[7] Although one may be tempted to suggest that this political violence has happened at the margins against marginalized peoples in the past, the capacity for political violence to erupt in the United States at an even greater level of intensity is considerable. Ever since Columbine in 1999, mass shootings have scarred the American landscape on a frequent and bloody scale. Increasingly, these shootings are overtly motivated by white supremacist or heterosexist ideologies, such as the mass shootings at Mother Emanuel A.M.E. Church in Charleston, the Tree of Life Synagogue in Pittsburgh, the Pulse nightclub in Orlando, and the spa shootings in the Atlanta area. At the same time, many shootings seem entirely random; they are simply citizens killing fellow citizens: Columbine, Sandy Hook, Parkland, Las Vegas. To the rest of the world, there is clearly something amiss in American society, but by the reactions from American politicians, one would hardly suspect there is a problem. Politicians have done little to prevent such shootings or abate the violence.

Weapons have only become more readily available and publicly displayed with increasing frequency, organization, and belligerency. Across the country, armed militias have operated with virtual impunity, which was on display as early as 2016 in the acquittal of the leaders of the armed occupation of the Malheur National Wildlife Refuge in Oregon.[8] For all those under the illusion that the violent language surrounding gun rights was merely metaphorical, the white nationalist rally in Charlottesville in 2017 should have stripped away such naiveté. Instead, what the American people got and what will be remembered by all was the president's enabling language asserting that there were "some very fine people on both sides,"[9] although one side was responsible for Heather Heyer's death and espoused an ideology of hatred and bigotry. The weaponry on display and the bellicosity in the air were more than a warning.

Throughout 2020, such intimidation became more prevalent and functioned as a political tactic at state houses around the country. In Virginia on January 20, 2020, masked (before COVID-19 mask mandates) and heavily armed gun-rights protesters gathered outside the state capitol where legislators were debating gun reform. At the gun-rights rally held about ten days later in the Kentucky State House, heavily armed and masked protesters were allowed to bypass metal detectors and brandish semi-automatic weapons.[10] In one of the more frightening episodes, right-wing, anti-government extremists plotted to abduct, put on trial and sentence Michigan Governor Gretchen Whitmer; though the conspiracy was revealed and foiled prior to launching, Trump downplayed the event and continued to criticize Governor Whitmer and the election results in Michigan.[11] None of this troubled Trump, who in the first presidential debate of 2020, little more than a month before the election, told the Proud Boys to "Stand back and stand by." The Proud Boys and other far-right extremists responded with enthusiasm. The natural result of all this was the assault against the Capitol on January 6, 2021, which should have surprised no one.[12] Elections have not yet been directly targeted, and political violence has been sporadic, but the violence and intimidation surrounding the 2020 election can be easily replicated in future elections. The title of this chapter seems like a painfully obvious point, and yet we are currently allowing armed political gangs to organize and operate with increasing belligerency in the United States. Firm, yet thoughtful, actions need to be taken to dismantle militias before they become any more powerful.

Chapter 14

INSTITUTIONS MAY NOT BE ABLE TO SAVE THE REPUBLIC

Over the centuries, Rome developed a deep sense of trust and confidence in its political institutions. Like clockwork, elections were held, wars were waged and won, elected officials consulted the senate, and the Romans prospered. Sure, there was disagreement, partisanship, divisions between rich and poor, and hotly contested elections, but there was also stability. Institutions, however, such as deliberative bodies, legal systems, and civic traditions can only bear so much strain. They can prop up a political community in conflict for only so long before they become torn and ultimately collapse under the weight of neglect and abuse. Rome in the late 50s was a poorly functioning political state, a very powerful state no doubt, but one barely able to hold an annual election. In 54 BCE, the candidates for consul participated in bribery, and consequently 53 BCE began with an interregnum, which lasted until July 53 BCE when consuls were finally elected. Typically, Roman consuls were elected in the July before they entered office in January; the consuls of 53 BCE were thus elected a full year after they should have been. The next year also began with an interregnum and ended with Pompey being elected sole consul as mentioned in the previous chapter. The elections for 51 and 50 BCE did proceed much more smoothly than the previous two years, but Rome was on shaky ground for determining how to handle Caesar's return from Gaul at the head of a triumphant army.

By the late 50s BCE, the Roman Republic was in such a debilitated state that it was no longer able to address the most pressing concerns of the day without violence and rancor. In 50 BCE, a concern that had been looming was now front and center. For years, everyone in Rome knew that at some point (the date was actually disputed), Caesar would be returning from Gaul, where he was systematically defeating his opponents. The natural question for Caesar and the Roman political class was—what to do with Caesar when he returned? Individuals and institutions had time to ponder this question. At stake was whether Caesar should be allowed to run in absentia for consul in 49 BCE, a right that had been granted to him in 52 BCE. If Caesar won the election, he would be shielded from his enemies, who wanted to charge him for political violations as consul in 59 BCE and then as general in Gaul. Rome proved incapable of resolving this dispute and marched in folly to war.[1]

The senate had taken a very adversarial approach to Caesar, who had supporters among the tribunes to veto any legislation contrary to his interests; meanwhile Pompey, Rome's counterweight to Caesar, refused to publicly support a solution. Pompey had his own authoritarian tendencies and was viewed by many, most conspicuously Cato, as an alternative to Caesar only out of necessity. In late 50 BCE, the tribune Gaius Scribonius Curio, Caesar's ally, put forth a proposal that both Pompey and Caesar lay down their arms; the senate passed the proposal overwhelmingly, 370–22, but the minority would win the day as the consul Gaius Claudius Marcellus voided the proposal. Then without any authorization, he took a sword to Pompey and asked him to take command of all forces in Italy to defend Rome. Pompey fatefully accepted, and in January 49 BCE, Caesar marched his army into Italy and on to Rome. Aside from the anonymous 22 senators who voted against the laying down of arms, it is unclear who preferred war to peace. Clearly the vast majority of senators wanted peace; Pompey and Caesar both had as much to lose in a civil war as to win, and there are indications that both made efforts in good faith to avoid it, sending proposals back and forth as the deadline neared. Nonetheless, Rome and its institutions—senate and elected officials—were unable to prevent it. Civil war was not inevitable; it could have been avoided, but the Romans were unable and unwilling to achieve an alternative.[2]

The United States faces its own consequential decisions, yet there seems little indication that its institutions, as venerable as they are, can handle the challenge. For nearly a decade now, Congress has struggled simply to agree to pay the bills. Budget debates and the question of raising the debt ceiling have crippled the government nearly every year in recent memory. Elected leaders who shut down the government rather than pay the expenses they voted to incur commit a scandalous abdication of duty. In 2018, the president, whose party controlled both houses of Congress, decided to shut down the government because he had not received funding to build a wall along the Mexican border. He stated that he was proud to do so until he received the funding (despite promising during his campaign that Mexico would pay for the wall).[3]

With an executive branch that is willing to shut down the government or declare a national emergency when Congress does not pass the laws it wants, one might be inclined to turn to the legislative branch for principled action on behalf of the common good, but Congress is little consolation. Neither party in Congress has an allegiance to their branch of government as a check on executive power. Partisanship would be more understandable if it were matched by competence, but that is not the case either; both parties can barely accomplish their agendas even when they have a supermajority and control of the White House. The Senate, which modestly calls itself "the world's greatest deliberative body," is hamstrung by the filibuster, which has blocked necessary legislation supported by both a majority of senators and American citizens. The bill to establish an independent investigation into the January 6 insurrection failed in the Senate despite the 54 to 35 bipartisan vote because of a Republican filibuster.[4] While Republican lawmakers were overly adulatory towards Trump and still seem incapable of putting country over party, Democrats have been disorganized and weak-willed. The Democrats, while controlling both houses of Congress, could barely pass a health care bill under President Obama in 2009–10 before the Republicans took back control of Congress. The Republicans for their part, despite their many votes to repeal the Affordable Care Act, could still not do so when they controlled both houses of Congress and the presidency.[5] To avoid the filibuster and pass important and necessary pieces of legislation, such as the Affordable Care Act and more recently the Coronavirus Aid, Relief, and Economic Security Act (CARES Act), Congress has had to resort to the reconciliation process.[6] We are now in a situation where arduous and difficult processes are required to pass desperately needed legislation, while any single senator, without stating a reason can declare a filibuster with relative ease and thereby essentially veto any bill.

The Late Roman Republic never endured a plague or pandemic that was of a scale to cause political upheaval.[7] In this way at least, the Romans were fortunate.[8] Devastating plagues would come to Rome, but that would not be until the reigns of Marcus Aurelius (160–181 CE) and Justinian (526–565 CE); by then Rome had no resemblance to a democracy.[9]

The United States has been profoundly challenged by the coronavirus pandemic and found greatly wanting. If the pandemic offered an opportunity for Americans to come together against a common threat, the opportunity was missed in a historic failure. A nation that appeared and boasted to be the richest and most powerful country in the world has been revealed as divided and unprepared for a crisis of this magnitude. Former President Trump and congressional leaders failed to take the virus seriously enough soon enough. America's unwillingness to invest in its community health infrastructure resulted in an inability to create and administer a test for the virus.[10] Although scientists were able to develop a vaccine in record time and deserve credit for doing so, the United States had no effective way to deploy the vaccine, which was delayed or dumped onto states with few resources for administering it. In both cases, testing and vaccination, there was ample time to prepare and act decisively, but the US political and health systems bungled the opportunity and wasted the interval.

The virus has exacerbated all of America's divisions: racial injustice, economic inequality, and political polarization foremost among them.[11] Although tens of millions of Americans have caught the virus and hundreds of thousands have lost their lives, the pandemic quickly became politicized. Protests against mask mandates and stay-at-home orders erupted across the country. Trump used racist language to describe the virus, and not surprisingly violence against Asian Americans and Pacific Islanders dramatically increased.[12] In response to shelter-in-place orders as a result of COVID-19, armed men protested in the Michigan State House and outside the private residence of Ohio Department of Health Director Amy Acton.[13] Not wearing a mask became a political statement in spite of the evidence that doing so greatly reduced the spread of the virus. No doubt, the pandemic has brought enduring changes to the United States and much of the world.[14]

At times of crisis, there is often a summoning of solidarity in the name of the common good. We even take such disasters out of our hands and call them an act of God, since no human can be blamed. This is the right and proper response. The need to think of others is real, and certainly times of crisis require all of us pulling together to see us through. But disease and natural disasters are not simply the act of God; whatever the origins of the crisis, humanity has the power to mitigate or exacerbate it. The call for the common good can also ring hollow for many if it is sounded only when the affluent come into danger or risk losing financially. If a society has accepted gross economic inequality, if it has functioned on the principle of private gains and public losses, if it has marginalized groups of people and ignored their pleas for a more just society including accessible and affordable health care, then calls for coming together, however real and necessary, seem quite the opposite of the common good and appear more like hypocrisy. Those who have already been alienated and abused by the health system will be slow to heed the call for vaccinations.[15] The common good needs to be the common good all the time, not just when there is a crisis.

At the time of this writing, the pandemic is surging due to the Delta variant, and it is uncertain when it may abate. An account detailing how the United States came together to defeat COVID-19 seems improbable; more likely, it will record that we botched the response and the pandemic only aggravated the divisions in society rather than healed them.[16] In addition to COVID-19, grave matters still confront the United States and the world, most acutely racial injustice and the climate crisis, to which could be added the opioid epidemic, growing economic inequality, and the rise of violence throughout the country. These challenges are interrelated and not easily solved. There is much evidence to suggest that the US government is not merely unwilling but also increasingly incapable of addressing the fundamental concerns of its citizens.

Chapter 15

A TYRANT BACKED INTO A CORNER IS A DANGER TO THE REPUBLIC

Traditionally in the Roman Republic, a conquering commander would have returned to the city amidst great fanfare in the hopes of being honored with a triumph, a grand parade through the streets of Rome. Yet Romans took care that the triumphant commander remained aware of his limitations by having an attendant ride on the triumphal chariot whispering in his ear, "Remember that you are not a god." The general would then become a private citizen again and likely take their place in the senate.[1]

Although he certainly merited a triumph, Caesar's return was different for several reasons. First, Rome was in no state to properly handle the return of a victorious general of Caesar's stature. It had been riven by too much violence, corruption, and partisanship. Rome was unable to find a creative way to reintegrate Caesar. Second, Caesar had ambitions; he was not returning to go into retirement or simply join the senate.[2] He had proven himself the greatest general of his generation and was intent on preserving his status. Lastly, Caesar had political enemies and he had engaged in a number of questionable actions both as consul and general. Whether or not his opponents could have succeeded in convicting him of any crimes is uncertain, nonetheless, Caesar claimed that if he were not able to move directly into another office, the consulship, he would be legally vulnerable to his enemies. If he remained an elected official, he would be immune from prosecution. Caesar's enemies may have been correct in claiming they had a legal case against him, but this in turn granted Caesar the cover to maintain that he had no other option than to remain in office or, denied that, to use force to protect himself. Caesar employed this rhetorical argument so effectively that it has even deceived many modern historians who argue that Cato and his supporters pushed Caesar into a corner. Caesar's wealth and popularity strongly militate against the idea that he had much to fear from a handful of cantankerous senators. Caesar was flush with cash enough to bribe whomever he needed and had support from his veterans to intimidate whenever necessary, not to mention his immense popularity. When the senate refused to grant him the option of running for consul in absentia, Caesar and his supporters argued that he had no other alternative but to protect himself by marching his army on Rome.

With a critical distance, later writers, such as Lucan,[3] would note the folly of having a highly competent general accompanied by battle-tested legions march on Rome to fight their fellow-citizens at a time when Rome's eastern frontier, following Crassus's humiliating defeat, lay exposed and its military standards were held in the possession of its enemies the Parthians. If Rome had the military resources and a first-rate military commander, there was certainly a frontier to defend and an opportunity to retaliate against an enemy. Caesar himself, once he had defeated his political enemies in Rome, was preparing for just such a campaign when he was assassinated in 44 BCE. Rather than pursue the option of tasking Caesar with some suitable undertaking, defending the eastern border against the resurgent Parthians for example, Rome and its allies would spend the next five years (49–45 BCE) engaging in an unnecessary and bloody civil war all around the Mediterranean. There would be no winners. Following his loss to Caesar at Pharsalus, Pompey was assassinated as he tried to seek refuge in Egypt (48 BCE). Caesar's bitter enemy Cato chose to commit suicide rather than surrender to Caesar following his victory at Thapsus in Africa (46 BCE). Even Caesar would be dead by early 44 BCE, assassinated by many of his former opponents whom he had pardoned. Caesar and his opponents had largely considered their own advantage in arguing over who deserved what rewards, but in doing so they lost sight of the greater good. Rome in the year 50 BCE also reminds us of the dangers in not thinking creatively for solutions and of the lengths to which a tyrannical politician will go to pursue his ambitions and avoid prosecution.

Like Rome and its treatment of consuls, the United States has a tradition of not indicting a sitting president with a crime. The Department of Justice holds the opinion that a sitting president is not amenable to indictment and criminal prosecution, that is, if the president commits a crime, it is not a legal matter, but rather a political matter to be addressed by Congress through the impeachment process.[4] Many Americans may be shocked to learn that, in effect, a sitting president is above the law. Though this is debatable constitutionally, it is the currently accepted practice which informed Special Counsel Robert Mueller's investigation and report on Donald Trump. As we are learning, this is not an academic question. Mueller testified to Congress that Donald Trump, had he not been president, could be indicted as a private citizen for his actions.[5] Donald Trump in all likelihood committed obstruction of justice and conspiracy, crimes worthy of indictment, but there was no indictment. Under current practice, a president is legally immune so long as he remains in office; once he leaves office, he is open to legal prosecution. While the idea that a sitting president is de facto above the law may be offensive, if not dangerous, a troubling consequence of this policy is that it creates a perverse incentive for a sitting president to take radical steps to remain in office. Therefore, we should not have been surprised that Trump took extraordinary measures to remain in office and avoid prosecution. One could rightfully conclude that this reality made the case for impeachment proceedings all the more compelling. A legitimate way to read Trump's insistence that the election of 2020 was stolen and his incitement of an attempted coup on January 6 was that he wanted to stay in office to avoid legal prosecution.

Whether or not Donald Trump will be prosecuted now that he is out of office remains an open question. To date he has not been, and some cases have been dropped, such as the investigation of "Hush-Money" payments to Stormy Daniels.[6] The Department of Justice has requested that the case against Trump for the forced removal of protesters from Lafayette Square be dropped on the basis that the president is protected from lawsuits over actions taken by the police for the president's security.[7] Nonetheless, other cases move ahead; the New York attorney general has joined the criminal investigation into the Trump Organization, while Georgia prosecutors are investigating his efforts to overturn the election results there.[8] In addition, Rudy Giuliani's home and offices were searched and assets were seized for the inquiry into his possible role as an unregistered foreign agent.[9] Whatever the outcome of these and other cases, Donald Trump has exposed many of the legal (and possibly illegal) options that are available to a sitting president and the lengths one can go to in order to remain in office.

Chapter 16

THE REAL PROBLEM IS NOT SIMPLY A TYRANNICAL LEADER

Brutus and Cassius thought they were living under a tyrant, and for good reason, but not all Roman citizens and senators considered Caesar a tyrant. Not all of them were troubled by the fact that after first having himself elected dictator for a year (47 BCE), and then for ten years (46 BCE), Caesar had finally made himself dictator for life (45 BCE)—akin to making oneself a president for life, something that exists neither in reality nor previously in the political imagination. If any Romans were troubled, Caesar's supporters could point to the needs of the state, his vaunted clemency towards his enemies (in such contrast to the dictator Sulla), and his grand plans for Rome, such as his public works and proposed campaign against the Parthians. Such Romans traded their political integrity for private gain; they traded freedom for Caesar's beneficence. Never mind that Caesar, who once used the freedom of the tribunes to launch a civil war, was now suppressing the free speech and political action of the tribunes who dared to challenge him on political matters. Forget that Caesar had a statue of himself erected among the kings of Rome on the Capitoline or took extraordinary titles and offices.[1] Why oppose such troubling behavior when Caesar promised you an office for next year? When one can receive a public office by the fiat of the dictator without the bother of having to campaign for the votes of one's fellow citizens, why resist the breakdown of political freedom and the rule of law?

Yet many still believed in the traditions of the Republic and recognized that Caesar had in effect put an end to the Republic. What does one do when one recognizes that one is living under a tyrant? Such was the question Roman citizens, like Brutus and Cassius, faced. Greco-Roman political theory seemed to provide an answer—tyrannicide, or short of that expulsion of the tyrant and his family. Democratic Athens had been established when Harmodius and Aristogeiton killed the tyrant Hipparchus, or so the popular version of the story went.[2] They were subsequently hailed as tyrant slayers and champions of freedom. Athens sang their praises and erected statues in their honor, as did Rome where sculptures of the Athenian tyrannicides stood on the Capitol.

The Romans themselves had a strong tradition of expelling tyrants. When the Romans became tired of Tarquinius Superbus's crimes and outraged by the sexual violence of his son, they rallied together and drove out the royal family. Lucius Brutus, the Liberator, played a crucial role in this expulsion and the subsequent creation of the Republic. The memory of this event cast a long shadow over Roman history, and it was to this example of resistance that Cassius, Brutus, and their compatriots turned; it would be their own undoing.

The assassination of Julius Caesar has been dramatically told and closely analyzed for millennia. In all those retellings, perhaps it is Shakespeare who best encapsulates both the moral impulse and the failure of the undertaking.[3] In the first half of the play, Shakespeare makes clear the Roman tradition of freedom and anti-tyrannical sentiment. The events surrounding the Lupercalia festival in 44 BCE, at which Caesar modestly renounced the crown offered by his groveler Mark Antony, revealed Caesar's naked ambition to make himself the master of Rome. Caesar did not need a crown; he had already made himself dictator for life.[4] These outrages inspired the dramatic act of killing Caesar, a friend and fellow citizen, for a good Roman "would have brooked / th' eternal devil to keep his state in Rome / as easily as a king."[5] Yet the second half of Shakespeare's *Julius Caesar* makes clear the dangers and difficulties of taking such violent and decisive action. At first, reconciliation and amnesty were championed by all, but the publication of Caesar's will, designating Octavian, Caesar's great-nephew, as his heir, brought disruption to this settlement. Caesar's supporters, his adopted son Octavian (the future Augustus) and Mark Antony foremost among them, raised armies to commence another round of civil war; Brutus and Cassius for their part did likewise.

Shakespeare reminds his readers that killing a tyrant does not heal the divisions within society and may even exacerbate them. For tyrants do not arise in a vacuum; they are a product of forces at work in the larger society. A hundred years of political turmoil had produced Caesar. Removing Caesar did not remove the causes that created him. Violence not only turned out to be a horrible and ineffective response, but it also failed to address the actual problem—a broken political system. Consequently, the violence continued for another generation and peace only came with an autocrat.

The best and easiest way to remove a tyrant is never to allow a tyrant to come to power. The Romans missed that opportunity time and time again over the preceding decades as they adopted a hyper-partisan political culture and surrendered their commitment to the common good.

In the United States, there are several mechanisms for removing an incompetent or tyrannical president. The first is through elections, which are the best and most respected way to remove an aspiring tyrant. Elections, however, have become an uncertain mechanism, for since 2000 they have become suspect and are open to manipulation at home and from abroad. There is also no longer a guarantee that an incumbent will observe the outcome of an election. In 2016, Trump argued that the result could not be trusted even in an election that he won. There are term limits to the office of the president, and one could hope that a tyrannical president would observe the constitutionally mandated term limit, but Trump stated that his followers might want him to remain in office beyond two terms, even before his election for a second term.[6]

There is also the option of impeachment, which the Constitution legally mandates when the president has committed high crimes and misdemeanors. Yet impeachment has been tried and failed twice, and as we have witnessed, impeachment has the drawback of being politically divisive, even if legally appropriate. Congressional lawmakers of both parties historically have shown little willingness to impeach a president from their own party and have rather demonstrated that they will maintain the utmost loyalty. Despite the direct threat to their lives on January 6, Republican legislators stood by Trump during his second impeachment; only ten Republican representatives voted to impeach Trump, and seven Republican senators voted to convict Trump.[7] A failed impeachment even has the potential to expand the limits of presidential power. A US president now apparently has the power to invite foreign powers to interfere with US elections and can incite with impunity his followers to storm the legislature. The precedent has been set; the threat of impeachment may no longer effectively exist. Trump was certainly not curbed by his first impeachment; rather he and his enablers, Rudy Giuliani foremost among them, saw the trial as an acquittal and a vindication of their actions. They punished those who testified against the president, such as Lieutenant Colonel Alexander Vindman. Moreover, Trump himself made us aware of the danger of impeaching the president and failing, retweeting *New York Times* White House correspondent Peter Baker's citation of Emerson's wisdom, "Ralph Waldo Emerson seemed to foresee the lesson of the Senate Impeachment Trial of President Trump. 'When you strike at the King,' Emerson famously said, 'you must kill him.'"[8] Following his acquittal in his second impeachment trial, Trump stated, "MAGA has only just begun."[9]

Short of the physical violence that Trump alluded to in his tweet and that the Romans have taught us the limitations of, there is one final option, which is also divisive and personally dangerous—peaceful public protest as a demonstration of public opinion. Public support is where Brutus and Cassius failed. Caesar enjoyed widespread support among Romans; rather than cultivating their own public support, Cassius and Brutus acted as independent agents assuming public opinion would rally around them after the assassination. American citizens still have the right to assemble publicly. There is the danger of arrest and violence—exacerbated by America's liberal gun laws—but a public demonstration of opposition has the potential to strengthen the mandate inherent in an election or a vote of impeachment.

There was great opposition to President Trump, but much of it was passive and there was little indication the American people were willing to assemble in a sustained manner, sporadic protests aside, until the late spring of 2020. The opposition to Trump wanted to rely on an election, impeachment, or the Constitution to do the heavy lifting. The murder of George Floyd, however, has given birth to a movement that has become a sustaining force not only to create racial justice but also to secure votes and elections, a not unrelated concern. The Black Lives Matter movement has brought people into the streets. These protests, though focused on the deaths of Black Americans, have had far-reaching ramifications for American democracy, which we are only beginning to understand. The African American community has suffered disproportionally from the coronavirus pandemic and stood to lose still more with the reelection of Donald Trump, yet in the call for justice for Black Americans, there is greater justice and freedom for us all, a lesson White Americans would do well to remember.

Behind any of these mechanisms for removing the president from office is the simplistic idea that the president is the problem. Indeed, Trump has been part of the problem, but even though he lost the 2020 election, there is little indication that American society will revert to its traditional political customs. The difficulties before us are much greater than a single politician, and it is much bigger than our political opponents, whoever they may be—liberal or conservative. Moreover, the crisis of American democracy has been decades in the making.[10] The increase in economic inequality and the intransigence of racism may be the primary obstacles to a healthy democracy, but more are easily added, such as complacency around climate change and access to guns and a whole host of polarizing social issues. A single election will not be enough to resolve our differences or to address the problems that confront us.

Chapter 17

FREE SPEECH CAN DISAPPEAR

In the 20 years since his suppression of the Catilinarian Conspiracy as consul in 63 BCE, Cicero had a checkered political career: exile at the hands of Clodius for his execution without trial of the citizen-conspirators, an uneasy accommodation with Caesar and Pompey after his recall, a lukewarm involvement in the civil war, and years in solitude composing philosophical tracts. As if throwing off 20 years of malaise, Cicero propelled himself into events following the assassination of Caesar. Cicero was not a party to the assassination, but he wasted no time in praising the tyrannicides and the newly asserted liberty. He was now the elder statesmen for a new generation of political leaders; most of his contemporaries had died either from age or from the violence of the civil wars.[1]

Cicero publicly aligned himself with Brutus and Cassius and sought to take under his wing Octavian, Caesar's grandnephew and adopted son, a political neophyte, though wise and ruthless beyond his years. In late 44 and early 43 BCE, the senate, led by Cicero, attempted to turn Octavian to their side and against Mark Antony. For a brief time, this strategy was successful, but Cicero would soon learn what many others have, that a "fateful alliance," rather than caution or outright opposition, with an ambitious, yet inexperienced, political outsider can fail tragically.[2] Cicero viciously tore into Antony in his famous *Philippics*, 14 speeches named after the orations against King Philip II of Macedonia by the Athenian orator Demosthenes. The speeches (some were published without being delivered) called Antony every name in the book—a drunkard, a gambler, and a whore-monger. Whether one agreed with Cicero or not, such language was in 43 BCE standard fare for how Romans frequently spoke and wrote about rival politicians. Simply put, Rome enjoyed free speech, lots of it. When Cicero composed his speeches and philosophical tracts, some of the most influential writings in Latin and European literature, no doubt he thought a great deal about what people would think of them—would his words be persuasive, would they stand up to his reputation, would they have their intended effect upon his audience? We can never be certain if Cicero ever thought about whether his words would get him imprisoned, exiled, or killed; given the ferocity with which Cicero attacked his political enemies, it seems that this was not foremost in his mind.

While this radical free speech had pertained for all of Cicero's life up to this point, things had changed. The senate's attempt to court the young Octavian failed when a senatorial army led by Octavian and the consuls Aulus Hirtius and Gaius Vibius Pansa defeated Antony at Mutina in April of 43 BCE. Although the senatorial army was victorious, both Hirtius and Pansa died as a result of the fighting; some suspected foul play, but in the end, Octavian was now alone at the head of a victorious army.[3] The senate muffed the ensuing negotiations, and Octavian marched his army on Rome to claim the consulship at the age of 19; he then marched north again to form an alliance with Mark Antony.[4] The alliance, which included a third man, Marcus Aemilius Lepidus, a Caesarian general, drew up proscription lists of their enemies in the tradition of Sulla; they had learned from the mistake of Caesar, whose pardoned enemies in turn assassinated him. Antony, Octavian, and Lepidus were determined to have as few surviving enemies as possible. The proscription lists granted a reward to anyone who hunted down any of the named individuals; those on the lists could be taken either alive or dead. Antony, incensed by Cicero's attacks in the *Philippics*, put Cicero's name on the list; Lepidus and Octavian, Cicero's former protégé, did not protest.[5]

Cicero was at a loss for what to do. He could hold out in his villa until the assassins arrived or he could race to join Brutus and Cassius. Cicero never liked warfare and political hesitation was part of his personality. He set out too late for Cassius and Brutus. When the assassins caught up to his carriage along the road, he is said to have merely stuck his head out the window and accepted his own death. His head and hands were brought to Rome and were nailed to the rostra, the speaker's platform in the forum, as an immediate lesson to all others that such outspokenness would no longer be tolerated. His death was a blow to Cassius, Brutus, and others hoping to restore some semblance of the Republic. For many of his opponents, who esteemed him even in disagreement, his brutal murder seemed excessive.[6] But there was no mistake to be made; when Antony had Cicero killed for his caustic orations, freedom of speech died with him. Romans henceforth would always have to consider their words carefully, and many would pay with their lives for not adhering to the emperor's desires.[7] It happened rather quickly, but its result was decisive—the principle of free speech would not recover on a broad scale in Western Europe for centuries.

In the United States, we are fortunate to have freedom of speech inscribed in the Constitution, and for centuries Americans have relied on this right to speak truth to power, satirize their politicians, and pursue their political agendas with little serious worry about imprisonment or execution. Certainly, there have been moments when speech was suppressed; over the centuries Rome had these moments too. We know that women and people of color in the United States have not enjoyed the full protection of the law as White men have. Not every judge and jury calls things as the law dictates, and there are many gray areas, but free speech has been a hallmark of American political life, and the First Amendment is a principle to call upon when free speech has been violated.

A central tenet of free speech is the freedom of the press, which has often wrangled with the leading politicians of the day. It is a trope of American politics that politicians dislike and distrust the press. Yet some politicians, such as Presidents Reagan, Clinton, and Obama in recent memory, have been able to use the press to their advantage and deflect criticism. One senses, however, that such back and forth between politicians and the press has taken on a new hostility. Trump labeled mainstream news media "fake news" and the "enemy of the people," always violent terminology.[8] Any news story that did not show Trump in a positive light became a lie. Even more, individual members of the press have been demonized and attacked, physically and verbally. In June 2018, Jarrod Ramos attacked and killed five staff members at the *Capital Gazette*.[9] Hostility towards the press has not been limited to Trump. Then candidate for the US House of Representatives, Greg Gianforte was convicted of assault against Ben Jacobs, a reporter for *Guardian*, whom Gianforte body-slammed.[10] Although Gianforte was sentenced to community service for his violent attack, he was also elected to represent Montana in Congress; in 2020 he was elected governor of Montana.

Such actions and language have devastating effects on free speech and the freedom of the press. By the end of Trump's presidency, journalism and free speech both in the United States and around the world had suffered greatly with unprecedented numbers of journalists assaulted and arrested.[11] During the attack on the Capitol on January 6, journalists were threatened and detained by the mob and had their equipment vandalized.[12] Despite this demonization, Americans for now still enjoy a robust freedom of speech, but so did the Romans up until it was swiftly and violently stripped away. Until that time, the Romans had a clear understanding of the power of public speech. Their education was designed to inculcate the ability to speak publicly. For the Romans, to speak in public was to act. We often make a distinction between mere words and productive action; this is a false dichotomy, which allows Donald Trump, on the one hand, to incite a coup and be let off the hook because he was merely speaking, while on the other hand, the rest of us are silenced because we accept that words do not matter, only actions do. We have forgotten that to speak is to act. Use your voice while you still can to support free elections, oppose corruption and oppression, and advocate for the common good.

Chapter 18

THE CRISIS CAN BE MANUFACTURED TO CONTINUE

The fifteen years following Caesar's assassination were a period of continued instability for Rome, as his successors fought among themselves for supremacy. The Roman people learned a difficult truth—Caesar was not the last tyrant. The Republic was in its last gasps, and if it were to survive it would be dependent on the armies of Brutus and Cassius, but even their victory was uncertain to secure the future of the Republic given all that had happened. In their absence from Rome, Antony, Octavian, and Lepidus formalized their alliance, often called the Second Triumvirate by modern historians. In November 43 BCE, this triumvirate received official status when a law was passed through the assembly of the people granting them a five-year period to put the state in order, which included the authority to make laws, appoint public officials, and allot provinces to governors. There were still elections in Rome, but they were merely affirmations of candidates put forward by the triumvirs, who designated public officials several years in advance, following Caesar's precedent. Even the consuls were now under their authority. One of their first orders of business was to draw up the proscription lists that allowed their opponents, such as Cicero, to be killed without penalty and their property confiscated. Julius Caesar was declared a god by the senate on January 1, 42 BCE, which made Octavian, his adopted son, the son of a god. Caesar's divinization was unprecedented; not since Rome's dim origins had any Roman been made a god, but the Romans would get used to the idea of emperors becoming divine upon their death. Octavian had his own aspirations.[1]

Cassius and Brutus were still in the east with a great many legions, which they had built up over the course of two years. The Triumvirate would need to confront them, which they did at Philippi in the autumn of 42 BCE. Antony and Octavian narrowly emerged victorious. Octavian showed no mercy against his defeated enemies and even had Brutus decapitated, sending his head to Rome as an offering to Caesar. One could argue that the Republic stopped functioning in 49 BCE, but the defeat at Philippi certainly sounded its death knell. The battle of Philippi in 42 BCE represented the final time public armies would fight on behalf of the Republic.²

Although their ostensible enemies had been defeated in battle, Antony, Lepidus, and Octavian still retained broad authority. There was not a single Cincinnatus in the group and no discussion of laying aside their power now that their foes had been vanquished. One might assume that under the leadership of the now dominant triumvirate peace would prevail in the Roman world, at least amongst Romans, but in fact, the triumvirs maintained the state of crisis by squabbling amongst themselves and forming tentative alliances with the remnants of Brutus and Cassius's forces, the last true believers. In 40 BCE, the triumvirate was reorganized. The alliance was sealed with a marriage between Antony and Octavia, the sister of Octavian. Antony and Octavian also divided up the provinces again; Antony was to take the east, where he would meet and marry Cleopatra, while Octavian took much of the west, save Africa and the islands. In 37 BCE, the triumvirate was renewed, most likely through 33 BCE, but by 36 BCE Lepidus would no longer be a triumvir on account of a betrayal of Octavian.³ Rather than putting the state in order, Antony and Octavian became the two most powerful men, just like Pompey and Caesar before them, and predictably hostilities broke out between them.

Octavian's success in his conflicts, first with Caesar's assassins and then with his fellow triumvirs, relied on violence and military might, but he also had an uncanny ability to portray his opponents somehow other than fully Roman. Although Octavian effectively cast Cassius and Brutus as traitors, he most successfully portrayed Mark Antony as a non-Roman. Antony had taken up residence in the east and began an affair with the Egyptian Cleopatra; Antony and Cleopatra eventually married and had several children together, whom Antony recognized as legitimate, an uncustomary act for a Roman, making Octavian's argument to Romans suspicious of eastern customs even easier. In 34 BCE, Antony gave these children some of Rome's eastern territories, an event known as the Donations of Alexandria. Octavian took the unscrupulous step of seizing Antony's will and sharing it publicly, though it is uncertain whether Octavian presented it truthfully or forged part of it. The will included the damning clause that Antony desired to be buried in Alexandria. Other rumors circulated that Antony was to give Cleopatra the city of Rome and move the capital to Alexandria; in addition, Antony had adopted the eastern dress and was enslaved to Cleopatra, who ruled jointly with him.⁴ Octavian's propaganda prevailed in convincing the people of the western half of the empire that they were marching off to war against a foreign enemy. Octavian succeeded in wrangling a loyalty oath from the western half of the empire, which he promoted as a consensus of all citizens. The imposition of a loyalty oath is typical of authoritarian leaders. In time, the Roman emperors would all require public oaths of loyalty from the senate, military, and people; Octavian set the precedent in 32 BCE.[5]

The failure of the marriage of Antony and Octavia provided the pretext if any was needed. Octavian's forces met the armies of Antony and Cleopatra at Actium, off the west coast of Greece, in 31 BCE. Octavian routed Antony and Cleopatra, who fled back to Egypt where the pair would famously commit suicide, leaving Octavian sole master of the Roman world. Octavian returned triumphant to Rome in 29 BCE and took the name Augustus, the "revered one," in 27 BCE. Rome was now the autocracy it would remain for the rest of its history.[6]

The triumvirs did not create peace for Rome because they did not want peace for Rome; they wanted power for themselves, which entailed the perpetuation of civil strife. The decade and a half after Caesar's assassination was unprecedented for Rome; the perennial chaos and upheavals are a reminder that some political leaders thrive on chaos rather than stability. In the years since the 2000 presidential election and the attack of September 11, 2001, the United States has seen a relatively great deal of instability. The terror attacks brought a new sense of insecurity, and the resulting quagmires of Afghanistan and Iraq have done little to restore confidence in the government's ability to accomplish its stated goals. Environmental catastrophes have overwhelmed the United States—hurricanes Katrina, Sandy and Ida, forest fires in the west, drought and excessive heat in the south and flooding in the plains. During this time, mass shootings have become normal. Places that once seemed spaces of safety and peace, such as schools, houses of worship, nightclubs, and restaurants, have become places of terror and heightened danger. Racial injustice and disparities stubbornly persist. The Great Recession brought into the mainstream the economic insecurity that some communities had been experiencing for decades. Although the economy has recovered for some, many have not experienced the economic gains and feel they have been left behind. This is to say nothing of the coronavirus pandemic, which has intensified racial and economic inequality.[7] Despite the devastating effects of these crises, American citizens and their government have struggled to find any consensus on how to address them. Further, all of these crises have been exploited for private gain.

Like Octavian before him, Donald Trump is also a master at portraying his opponents as un-American. His most common rhetorical means for doing this are white identity and masculinity. In an infamous case while still candidate, Trump attacked Judge Gonzalo Curiel, who was presiding over the case against Trump University, because he had "an absolute conflict" on account of his "Mexican heritage"; Judge Curiel is a US citizen born in Indiana, but

Trump played to his supporters by casting Curiel as not a real American.[8] Trump's frequent references to the "China virus" rather than the coronavirus was a similar ploy, and one that fomented animosity and violence against Asian Americans and Pacific Islanders.[9] Likewise hyper-masculinity featured prominently in Trump's presidency.[10] For example, Trump appealed to outdated gender roles in an attempt to bolster his support from women at a campaign rally in Lansing, Michigan, proclaiming, "We're getting your husbands back to work." This statement might have been merely offensive had it not been made at a time when women were being driven from the workforce in great numbers on account of the pandemic and could have used support and policies from the president rather than misogynistic rhetoric.[11] Of course, Trump's performance of masculinity was displayed in his violent rhetoric against his female political opponents. During his campaign in 2016, Trump's rallies frequently resounded with chants of "Lock her up," referring to Hillary Clinton. In 2019, the chants had changed to "Send her back," referring to Rep. Ilhan Omar.[12] Trump's attacks on Rep. Ilhan Omar, a Muslim woman of color, were especially virulent. These divisive attacks succeeded in riling up his base and polarizing America and created an ever-changing news cycle that moved from outrage to outrage.

Trump has not only thrived on chaos but also has used it to cover his lies. As president, Trump survived any number of political crises that would have taken down most politicians, simply by creating another crisis, which compelled the American public to forget the previous scandal. Every week of the Trump presidency brought a fresh outrage—racially offensive comments (his frequent go-to), allegations of new corruption, the transgression of another revered custom, virulent attacks on his political enemies, and so on.[13] As journalists and politicians responded to one outrage, the president and his followers were already on to their next one. Authoritarian leaders attempt to colonize the mind of their subjects before they colonize the rest of the person. Trump did this very effectively. The QAnon conspiracy provides ample evidence of how such mental colonization can occur and its dangers.[14] History and reflection itself are acts of political resistance to leaders such as Trump. Many of those who supported President Biden did so in the hopes of a return to normalcy, but the United States seems to be at a point where disruption in itself has become a political strategy.

Chapter 19

THE REVOLUTION CAN BE ADVERTISED AS A RESTORATION

When Augustus was nearing his end, he wrote out a lengthy text of his deeds, the *Res Gestae*, literally, *The Things Done*. He then had this text inscribed throughout the empire in Latin and Greek. It is a long and unimaginative list of the temples he restored, his generosity towards the people, his conquests, and the ensuing peace. Although the *Res Gestae* contains many facts, and certainly other Romans had tomb inscriptions, nonetheless it is an inscription only an autocrat could write. In its opening lines, Augustus describes himself as a second Brutus the Liberator, boasting that he freed the Republic from the domination of a faction. He goes on to claim that following the civil wars, he restored the Republic to the senate and people of Rome.[1] Previously, Augustus had promised to restore the Republic upon Antony's return from the east; for this gesture, the people rewarded him with the office of tribune of the plebs for life. Suetonius writes that he intended to restore the Republic after he defeated Antony and then again once when he was terribly sick; neither time did he follow through.[2] Augustus also professed to have restored Rome through its buildings, claiming to have restored over 80 temples, but even this restoration was wrapped up in revolution, for Augustus claimed to have found Rome, a city of brick but left it a city of marble.[3]

Historians have debated what he meant by this claim and what he actually handed back that could count as restoring a republic to its people. Centuries ago, Tacitus presented the truth when he wrote that Augustus had taken everything under his power.[4] Despite Augustus's claims to have restored the Republic, he was actually a revolutionary. Once he was fully ensconced in power, he portrayed himself as a tolerant, benevolent leader, merely the first citizen (*princeps*). He could afford to be such a leader because he had seen to the death of many of his enemies; he had the money to seduce those willing to serve his interests; and most of all he had the legions. Augustus's approach was brilliant; unlike Caesar who made clear his power by having himself named dictator for life, a thoroughly radical and un-Republican position, Augustus merely used the veneer of the Republic to cloak his power.[5] It is no surprise that Caesar was assassinated shortly after becoming dictator for life, nor that Augustus died in his sleep at the age of 76. Although Augustus did take honorary titles, such as Augustus, *princeps*, and *imperator* (commander/emperor), he did not create any new political office for himself. He took some powers of the tribunes, such as the right to veto and pass legislation; he held the office of consul repeatedly. What was revolutionary about Augustus was that he generally held many of these powers concurrently—the tribunician powers and the consulship for example. However, Augustus put on a conservative persona. He avoided ostentatious displays of wealth; he encouraged and actively took part in traditional religious worship. He befriended poets and artists and built public works, including the rebuilding of the senate house. Augustus was also highly competent; he made good decisions and did not waste resources. In many ways, he was a just and sensible ruler.

Nonetheless, the state had undergone a revolution. A long list of Augustus's unprecedented maneuvers could be created, almost an antithesis of the *Res Gestae*; at *Annals* 1.10, Tacitus does his best to deconstruct the façade Augustus had created. Although the names of the magistrates stayed the same and elections continued, the vast majority of the candidates were approved by Augustus and the elections became a farce, mere routine. Augustus assumed the role of commander in chief of the military; the commanders in the provinces were merely his deputies and thereby became ineligible for any of the public recognition for victorious generals. Augustus held the reins of power just so, always allowing himself and his followers plausible deniability. If someone challenged his continuous holding of the consulship, he could merely claim that the people were the ones who elected him; moreover, Marius too held the consulship repeatedly. At least, he was not a sole consul like Pompey, or a dictator like Caesar. If push came to shove, he could also give up the consulship for a year, which would be seen as a grand display of republicanism, never mind that he could afford to do so because he had other levers of power on which to rely. He was granted many privileges, but he could always claim that the senate and people freely gave them to him and he did not actively seek them. In this way, Augustus carried out a revolution in the guise of a restoration.[6]

Trump's campaign slogan in 2016 was "Make America Great Again." All politicians claim they will make America great in some way, but Trump's "again" conveyed the most powerful part of his message. Trump promised to restore America to some unspecified golden age when things in America worked a certain way, undoubtedly a time when the power of wealthy White men held sway. Unlike many presidential candidates, he did not make promises about a new future better than the past or the creation of a more perfect union. His America was great once, and he wanted to take Americans back there again. This message was an appealing one as the election demonstrated. Voters apparently believed Trump when he made his appeal to the past, despite the fact that he went on to break an untold number of precedents both as a candidate and as a president, his disregard for the truth being foremost among them.[7] His slogan was very clever though, because it provided him the veneer of a traditional conservative, which he clearly was not, while he made unprecedented moves on the side. If anyone challenged him, he could simply point to the hat. Leaders like Augustus and Trump are capable of living in a tension: they claim to be better and more capable than all the rest, but they also assert that they are doing nothing new. For many, this seems contradictory, but for Augustus and Trump there is no difficulty in being a restorer and a revolutionary at the same time. Claiming the one allows them to be the other.

Chapter 20

FREEDOM LOST CANNOT SO EASILY BE REGAINED

So what? So what if the Roman Republic fell and evolved into an autocracy? Well, first I hope to have shown that the fall of the Roman Republic offers us some warning signs of how republics in general can fall. Yet most of all, ancient Rome can show us what we have to lose. The Roman Republic, for all its failings (slavery, patriarchy, imperialism, inequality, etc.), allowed those counted among its citizens the freedom to think, write, and speak what they wanted, to publicly gather and protest for greater rights, to elect their representatives and vote on their laws, to seek justice under the law, and to dream and advocate for a better society. Under the Empire, all of these freedoms were either sporadically tolerated, greatly curtailed or lost entirely, and once they were lost, they did not return. The Roman historian Tacitus states it most clearly when he writes that freedom and civic virtues are difficult to revive; the intellect and its pursuits are more easily oppressed than they are restored.[1]

Cicero's execution and the loss of free speech has already been discussed, but it is important to add that Romans continued to face punishment, including execution, for expressing their opinions. Tacitus records how under the emperor Tiberius in 25 CE, Cremutius Cordus was convicted and forced to commit suicide for his histories, in which he praised Cassius and Brutus; his books were burned as a further punishment.[2] In addition, speech was corrupted into flattery, as citizens rushed to obey in advance. Free speech declined not simply because the emperors condemned opposition material, but also because Romans tried to anticipate the emperor's desires, thereby engaging in ever-increasing self-censorship and adulation as they tried to outdo one another in their servility.[3]

Elections under Augustus had become a symbolic gesture, but Tiberius, his successor, eliminated public elections altogether when he transferred the selection of public officials from the people to the senate. Although Rome would continue to have consuls and tribunes, and all the other traditional offices for quite some time, they would no longer wield their traditional powers and functions and they would not be elected by the people. Tiberius did this with little fanfare, and it seems there was little opposition to their disappearance; it had been a long time since Rome had held meaningful elections. With the elections went the right of the people to pass legislation. The Roman people were no longer sovereign. The emperor now had that privilege.[4]

Under the Empire, the Roman senate did gain some powers, as it now chose public officials, under the oversight of the emperor of course, and its decrees took on the force of law. However, the senate became a shadow of its former self. A deliberative body that once oversaw Rome's growth from a city-state to a Mediterranean empire now spent much of its time trying to figure out how to please the emperor, who often grew weary of the flattery. The emperor Tiberius was accustomed to say when leaving the senate house, "O men prepared for servitude!"[5] The senate rarely undertook any business for which the emperor had not already expressed support.

Further, the Roman people and senate often became fools and victims to Augustus's successors. Caligula (37–41 CE) might not have ever nominated his horse for consul, as our sources suggest, but he did poison his second cousin Tiberius Gemellus, who had a rival claim to the throne. Rather than attend to the serious matters of government, Nero (54–68 CE) fancied himself an actual poet and actor and compelled audiences to endure his performances; once a woman was forced to give birth rather than leave his recitals. This is to say nothing of his many other excesses like engineering the murder of his mother. The emperor Domitian (81–96 CE) killed his political opponents and terrorized the senate.[6] The list of mockeries and atrocities committed by Augustus's successors could go on for many pages. The Roman historians of the empire, Tacitus, Suetonius, Dio, have compiled them for us to consult. Their writings are an argument for republicanism.

Some might object that although the emperors were bad for the elites who wrote those histories, nonetheless they improved life for the common people, but this is not true. The Roman revolution began with a tribune of the people trying to give land to the dispossessed; it ended with Augustus co-opting the elites with gifts and offices to make them amenable to his rule and dispensing with any radical plans. The poor of Rome at the time of Augustus's death (14 CE) were as poor as those in the time of Tiberius Gracchus's tribunate (133 BCE); the only difference was that they no longer had a credible way to advocate for changing the circumstances of their lives and were left to resort to shouting at the emperor when he appeared at the games. To be sure, there were good emperors from time to time—Vespasian, Trajan, Marcus Aurelius—but the law of autocracy held true: while some autocrats are competent and temperate, the bad autocrats are really bad and just as common.

What is more, republicanism and the freedoms it provided faded from the intellectual and political landscape of Western Europe for over a millennium. Yes, vestiges of republican thought survived and enclaves of republican states existed from time to time, but nothing on the scale of the Roman Republic. Much time and hard work, and many lives, would be sacrificed before republican and democratic forms of government were viable options for large populations in Western Europe. The founding of the United States, over 1800 years after the battle of Philippi, changed this and provided the evidence that with struggle a democratic republic could once again bring peace, justice, and prosperity to its citizens. Like the Romans, the United States has had its failings (slavery, patriarchy, economic inequality, racism); we are not as just and free as we think we are, but the United States has given ideas like freedom, equality, and justice a sustained fighting chance for its citizens and the world. What a loss it would be if the ideals of the Declaration of Independence, the Constitution, the Gettysburg Address, the "Letter from Birmingham Jail," and many other classics of democratic republicanism were discarded just so we can see our political opponents ridiculed and defeated. What a betrayal it would be of the revolutionary generation, those who died at Gettysburg and on the fields of Europe, the suffragettes, the striking workers, the civil rights activists, and all those others who devoted their lives to a better future for us all, if we traded their sacrifices for a political culture that turns our opponents into enemies, curtails freedom of speech, tolerates violence and intimidation, and delegitimizes elections. Even if our side "wins," what will we have won? We will have exchanged hope, idealism, and sacrifice for hate, cynicism, and complacency. The question is not simply whether our founding documents are true; the question is whether we still believe in those documents enough to sacrifice for the ideals they contain. Which side of history do we want to be on?

CONCLUSION

Julius Caesar, who is the most commonly identified Roman tyrant, did not transform Rome into an autocracy. Although Caesar played a crucial role in that transformation, Augustus, a generation later, is really the one who created and solidified autocracy at Rome. Moreover, the problem was greater than any one person or group of people and was decades in the making. Rome does not provide a model for a way out of this descent into autocracy. Just as Polybius pointed out that the Romans were not excluded from the law of *anacyclosis*, the rise and fall of states, so the United States is not excluded either. The danger for America is assuming that Trump was the source of our political problems. The republic of the United States has outlived the presidency of Donald Trump, though the dynastic aspirations of his children and their spouses should not be dismissed; Augustus's success where Caesar failed should give pause to anyone looking to celebrate Trump's departure from the White House.[1] Most certainly, the republic has not overcome the crises Trump exploited and accelerated. If the United States is going to outlive the next authoritarian candidate, whether from the left or the right, we will need to radically change our politics.[2]

The forces that Trump has brought into the light have been latent in the US political system for decades, if not from its origins: misogyny, xenophobia, racism, economic inequality. Trump did not invent them, though he kept alive and nourished these divisions for his own gain. Trump is no longer president, but our long-standing divisions are still with us waiting for someone to exploit them. In addition, Trump's reckless political behavior has provided precedents for any successors, who, regardless of political party, will find them hard to resist. Augustus succeeded where Caesar failed because he learned from Caesar's mistakes and exploited the political precedents established in the last century of the Republic. The real question is not what to do with a leader like Trump. The real question before us is what to do with our republic, which is greatly diminished. Over eighty million Americans voted for Joe Biden and nearly seventy-five million voted for Donald Trump. Whatever wishful thinking either party engages in, a sizable minority will be supporting the other party for the foreseeable future. Demographics alone will not change this; the departure of Donald Trump will not change this. As David Brooks wrote shortly after the election, "the other side is not going away."[3] It seems the United States will need to face down its demons, however painful an experience it may be.

There are at least four existential threats to American democracy: white supremacy, climate change, economic inequality, and political violence; these are not mutually exclusive concerns of course, but are in fact tightly bound together in complex ways. We will have to choose between a multicultural, multiracial democracy or White supremacy. We will need to work for environmental justice or accept the consequences of climate change denial. The United States can choose broad economic prosperity or the conflict that comes with economic inequality. In place of political violence and autocracy, we can have freedom and broad political participation founded on a rich sense of the common good.

I wish that I could provide examples from the last 100 years of the Roman Republic of those who successfully resisted, who stemmed the tide of economic inequality, violence and autocracy. I cannot. Not because the fall of the Roman Republic was inevitable. Nothing is inevitable. I cannot because they all failed however noble their efforts. In fact, many of the political leaders discussed here—Cicero, Cato, Caesar himself—did many good things on behalf of Rome, but they also participated in its decline. There are models indeed who resisted the autocracy of the Roman Empire; historians like Tacitus record their stories, but they succeeded only in showing that resistance to tyranny was possible and in providing a dim faith in republican government. We do not want only models of resistance after freedom is lost: we also need examples of those who maintained democracy and the common good.

For the republic of the United States to survive, we will need to become our own models. I cannot say what those models will look like, but I think it will require two actions—one abstract, one concrete. We will need to renew the social contract by appealing to the ideals of our founding documents and subsequent democratic tradition, not only because they will provide us with inspiration, but also because the ideals found in them give us our reasons for going on together. They answer the central question—why are we citizens with one another? Why have we formed a country together and live in solidarity with one another? There are many reasons—Trump has spent six years pointing them out every day—why we should not be in solidarity with one another. The United States, which is unique among nations so far as I know, finds its answer in the ideals of our founding documents—equality, life, liberty, justice for all. These are lofty and abstract ideals, but they are worth fighting for in the day to day.

The second action, which is concrete, is loving one another. I am not sure that we do currently. There is a lot of hatred and anger in the United States. We will have to find a way to defuse it, and even more, we will have to find a reason why to defuse it. From Abigail Adams to Malcolm X, from Cesar Chavez to George Washington, our republican ancestors have given us more than lofty words. The people just named are an incongruous group, but they have each contributed important pieces to the edifice of our republic (briefly: rights for women, African Americans and immigrants, and political forbearance), and even more they have passed on to us the mission to create a more perfect union. This is the act of love we need to engage in. This is the work that gives flesh to the ideals of our founding.

Perhaps it is rather sentimental to point it out, but unless we can find a reason why people in California and Alabama, or warehouse workers and professors, or gun-owners and pacifists, should love one another, then I fear we do not have much of a future together. If we have no interest in serving one another and if there is no good common among us, then we will likely fight over the greatest rewards. This is the example Rome provides us. Let us provide a different one.

NOTES

To the Reader

1. Roman historians generally divide Roman history into three periods based on the type of government that prevailed: the monarchy, the Roman Republic, and the Roman Empire. The term "Roman Empire" is not completely satisfactory as the Romans had a geographic empire during the Republic, but the term is used to designate the time period in which the Romans were ruled by an emperor. Sometimes the term "Principate" is used to designate the first two centuries of the Roman Empire in order to suggest that Rome was governed by its first citizen (*princeps*); by the third century CE, however, this concept no longer describes the Roman government, which became both more unstable and autocratic. In this book, I will use the terms Roman Republic and Roman Empire to refer to forms of government; when I refer to Rome's geographic empire, I will use the lower-case "empire."
2. For a detailed examination of the Roman constitution, see Andrew Lintott, *The Roman Constitution* (Oxford: Oxford University Press, 1999).
3. For this distinction, see James Madison's *Federalist* 10. Some take issue with this definition of a republic, such as William R. Everdell, *The End of Kings: Republics and Republicans* (New York: The Free Press, 1983), 1–15, who understands the primary importance of a republic to be the prevention of monarchy. I do not believe these are mutually exclusive, as representative democracy is one way to prevent autocracy.
4. For Cloelia, Cincinnatus, Camillus and the Twelve Tables, see Livy, *History of Rome* 2.13.6, 3.19–29, 3.34, 3.57, 5.19–55. Cincinnatus will be discussed further in Chapter 8. The reader should note that most ancient writings are typically referenced by book and chapter number, similar to the *Bible*; thus, 2.13.6 indicates book two, chapter thirteen, section six. Full citations to frequently referenced ancient authors can be found in the Bibliographic Note.
5. For studies on these works, see Danielle Allen, *Our Declaration: A Reading of the Declaration of Independence in Defense of Equality* (New York: Liveright, 2014); Ellen Carol Dubois, *Suffrage: Women's Long Battle for the Vote* (New York: Simon & Schuster, 2020); Garry Wills, *Lincoln at Gettysburg: The Words that Remade America* (New York: Simon and Schuster, 1992); D. D. Hansen, *The Dream: Martin Luther King Jr. and the Speech that Inspired a Nation* (New York: Harper Collins, 2003); G. Louis Heath, *Vandals in the Bomb Factory: The History and Literature of the Students for a Democratic Society* (Metuchen, NJ: Scarecrow Press, 1976). For these documents and others, see Kenneth Bridges, ed., *Freedom in America* (Upper Saddle River, NJ: Pearson Education, 2008).

6 For one example identifying Trump with Julius Caesar, see Tim Elliot, "America Is Eerily Retracing Rome's Steps to a Fall. Will It Turn Around before It's Too Late?," *Politico*, November 3, 2020, https://www.politico.com/news/magazine/2020/11/03/donald-trump-julius-caesar-433956.

Introduction: Why Rome?

1 Throughout I use "citizen" to designate someone who has the rights and responsibilities to participate freely in their government, in contrast to a "subject" who is governed by a political master, for example, a king, dictator, or a supreme leader. This usage is distinct from one that discriminates between "citizen" and "non-citizen," that is, those in the political community and those excluded from it.
2 For the question of whether the United States is or is not another Rome, see Sarah E. Bond, "Are We Romans?," *History from Below*, https://sarahemilybond.com/chicken-littles-are-we-romans/; Vaclav Smil, *Why America Is Not a New Rome* (Cambridge, MA: MIT Press, 2014); Cullen Murphy, *Are We Rome? The Fall of an Empire and the Fate of America* (New York: Mariner Books, 2008).
3 Global Slavery Index, https://www.globalslaveryindex.org; Kate Hodal, "One in 200 People Is a Slave. Why?," *Guardian*, February 25, 2019, https://www.theguardian.com/news/2019/feb/25/modern-slavery-trafficking-persons-one-in-200.
4 For the genocide of Native Americans, see Dee Brown, *Bury My Heart at Wounded Knee* (New York: Holt, Rinehart & Winston, 1970); Glenn T. Morris and Simon Maghakyan, "The U.S. Has Finally Acknowledged the Genocide of Armenians. What about Native Americans?," *Washington Post*, April 29, 2021, https://www.washingtonpost.com/opinions/2021/04/29/us-biden-armenian-genocide-native-americans-recognition/. For excellent studies on white supremacy and racial injustice in the United States, see Michelle Alexander, *The New Jim Crow: Mass Incarceration in the Age of Colorblindness* (New York: The New Press, 2012); Richard Rothstein, *The Color of Law: A Forgotten History of How Our Government Segregated America* (New York: Liveright, 2017); Charles W. Mills, *The Racial Contract* (Ithaca: Cornell University Press, 1997); Eddie S. Glaude Jr., *Democracy in Black: How Race Still Enslaves the American Soul* (New York: Crown Publishers, 2016); Ibram X. Kendi, *Stamped from the Beginning: The Definitive History of Racist Ideas in America* (New York: Bold Type Books, 2016).
5 Livy, *History of Rome* 1.49–60.

Chapter 1 Anacyclosis: no regime is exceptional and democracy is not inevitable

1 Tacitus, *Annals* 1.1.1.
2 Polybius, *Histories* 1.1, 3.5.
3 Plato, *Republic* 5.499a, *Laws* Book 3; Aristotle, *Politics* 4.8.1294a–4.9.1294b; Jacqueline de Romilly, *The Rise and Fall of States according to Greek Authors* (Ann Arbor: University of Michigan Press, 1991).
4 Polybius, *Histories* 6.1–57.
5 Polybius, *Histories* 6.57.
6 Pseudo-Sallust, *Second Letter to Caesar* 2.10.8; Livy, *History of Rome* preface 9; Lily Ross Taylor, *Party Politics in the Age of Caesar* (Berkeley: University of California Press, 1966).

7 For the idea of "successful assertions of popular sovereignty," see Robert Morstein-Marx, "'Cultural Hegemony' and the Communicative Power of the Roman Elite," in *Community and Communication: Oratory and Politics in Republican Rome*, ed. Catherine Steel and Henriette van der Blom (Oxford: Oxford University Press 2013), 29–47.
8 For the role American political parties play in rooting out extremists, see Steven Levitsky and Daniel Ziblatt, *How Democracies Die* (New York: Crown, 2018), 40–52.
9 Peter Wehner, "The GOP Is a Grave Threat to American Democracy," *The Atlantic*, April 26, 2021, https://www.theatlantic.com/ideas/archive/2021/04/gop-grave-thr eat-american-democracy/618693/; William Saletan, "Republicans still Sympathize with the Jan. 6 Capitol Insurrection," *Slate*, April 15, 2021, https://slate.com/news-and-politics/2021/04/republican-party-sympathize-capitol-insurrection.html.

Chapter 2 Mighty republics can fall because of slow corruption rather than dramatic revolutions

1 Appian, *Civil Wars* 1.121; Livy, *Periochae* 97; Robin Seager, *Pompey the Great*, 2nd ed. (Malden, MA: Blackwell, 2002), 30–39.
2 Augustus, *Res Gestae* 1.4; Livy, *Periochae* 119; Suetonius, *Augustus* 26.1; Appian, *Civil Wars* 3.88; Dio, *Roman History* 46.43–46; Alison E. Cooley, *Res Gestae Divi Augusti: Text, Translation, and Commentary* (Cambridge: Cambridge University Press, 2009), 113.
3 Augustus, *Res Gestae* 34.1, *rem publicam ex mea potestate in senatus populique Romani arbitrium*.
4 Tacitus, *Annals* 1.3.7–4.1.
5 Robin Bradley Kar and Jason Mazzone, "The Garland Affair: What History and the Constitution Really Say about President Obama's Powers to Appoint a Replacement for Justice Scalia," *New York University Law Review Online* 91 (2016): 53–114; Matthew Daly, "Who's a Hypocrite: GOP, Dems Debate Past Comments on Court," *Associated Press*, September 22, 2020, https://apnews.com/article/election-2020-ruth-bader-ginsburg-merrick-garland-elections-us-supreme-court-bb9932748b199f793cb2ccbef a713a5f.
6 Domenico Montanaro, "Why President Obama Campaigning for Clinton Is Historic," *NPR*, July 5, 2016, https://www.npr.org/2016/07/05/484817706/looking-back-at-a-century-of-presidents-not-campaigning-for-their-successor. For opposing viewpoints on Former President Obama's behavior, see Marc A. Thiessen, "Look Who's Shattering Presidential Norms Now," *Washington Post*, September 11, 2018, https://www.washing tonpost.com/opinions/democrats-like-to-talk-about-trump-breaking-norms-now-obama-is/2018/09/11/3cb66ef4-b5ff-11e8-a2c5-3187f427e253_story.html; Nicholas F. Jacobs, "Is Obama Breaking Norms as a Former President? Not Really," *Washington Post*, September 25, 2018, https://www.washingtonpost.com/news/monkey-cage/ wp/2018/09/25/obamas-returned-to-public-life-like-past-presidents-throughout-u-s-history/.
7 Rebecca Tan, Peter Jamison, Carol D. Leonnig, Meagan Flynn, and John Woodrow Cox, "Trump Supporters Storm U.S. Capitol, Shots, Tear Gas Fired," *Washington Post*, January 7, 2021. https://www.washingtonpost.com/local/trump-supporters-storm-capitol-dc/2021/01/06/58afc0b8-504b-11eb-83e3-322644d82356_story.html.
8 Stuart A. Wright, *Patriots, Politics, and the Oklahoma City Bombing* (Cambridge: Cambridge University Press, 2007); Lou Michel and Dan Herbeck, *American Terrorist: Timothy McVeigh and the Tragedy at Oklahoma City* (New York: Avon Books, 2002).

Chapter 3 A revered tradition of liberty can be exploited by authoritarians

1. For Roman hostility to the word "king," see Cicero, *Letters to Atticus* 8.11.2, *On the Republic* 2.30, *On Duties* 3.83; Sallust, *Jugurthine War* 31.7; Livy, *History of Rome* 2.1.9; Plutarch, *Poplicola* 12. For the more neutral sentiments of the Augustan poets, who lived and wrote under the authoritarian Augustus, see Robert J. Murray, "The Attitude of the Augustan Poets toward *Rex* and Related Words," *Classical Journal* 60.6 (1965): 241–46.
2. Justinian, *Institutes* 1.3; Charles Wirszubski, *Libertas as a Political Idea at Rome during the Late Republic and Early Principate* (Cambridge: Cambridge University Press, 1960), 1–3.
3. Thomas E. Strunk, *History after Liberty: Tacitus on Tyrants, Sycophants, and Republicans* (Ann Arbor: University of Michigan Press, 2017), 23–37.
4. Publilius Syrus, *Sententiae* 61, *beneficium accipere libertatem est vendere*; see also *Sententiae* 641 *rogare officium servitus quodammodo est*—"to ask for a favor is a form of servitude."
5. Caesar's motivations for beginning the civil war: Caesar, *The Civil Wars* 1.5–8, 22, *The African War* 22; Augustus's motivations: Augustus, *Res Gestae* 1.1. For the coinage of Brutus, see Dio, *Roman History* 47.25.3; Michael H. Crawford, *Roman Republican Coinage* (Cambridge: Cambridge University Press, 1987), 1:518, no. 508/3. For liberty and domination, see Tacitus, *Histories* 4.73.3.
6. For the rhetorical use and misuse of Roman *libertas*, see Ronald Syme, *The Roman Revolution* (Oxford: Oxford University Press, 1939), 154–56; Wirszubski, *Libertas as a Political Idea* 103–104; Valentina Arena, *Libertas and the Practice of Politics in the Late Roman Republic* (Cambridge: Cambridge University Press, 2012), 244–57.
7. Plato, *Republic* 8.562a–564a.
8. George Lakoff, *Whose Freedom? The Battle over America's Most Important Idea* (New York: Farrar, Straus, and Giroux, 2006); Eric Foner, *The Story of American Freedom* (New York: W.W. Norton, 1998). For the American understanding of liberty more recently following the terrorist attacks of September 11 and the presidency of Barack Obama, see Orlando Patterson and Ethan Fosse, "Stability and Change in Americans' Perception of Freedom," *Contexts* (Summer 2019), https://contexts.org/articles/stability-and-change-in-americans-perception-of-freedom/; Richard C. Leone and Gregory Anrig, eds., *Liberty Under Attack: Reclaiming Our Freedoms in an Age of Terror* (New York: Public Affairs, 2007).
9. Abraham Lincoln, *Lincoln's Selected Writings*, ed. David S. Reynolds (New York: W.W. Norton, 2015), 143. The italics are printed in Reynolds's text.

Chapter 4 Economic inequality drives civil strife

1. See Adrian K. Goldsworthy, *The Punic Wars* (London: Cassell, 2001); Robin Waterfield, *Taken at the Flood: The Roman Conquest of Greece* (Oxford: Oxford University Press, 2014).
2. For sumptuary legislation, see Emanuela Zanda, *Fighting Hydra-like Luxury: Sumptuary Regulation in the Roman Republic* (London: Bloomsbury, 2013), especially 49–71.
3. Livy, *History of Rome* preface 11–12; Polybius, *Histories* 6.57, 18.34–35; Sallust, *Catiline's War* 11.4–5.
4. See, for example, Livy, *History of Rome* 30.45.3, 31.20.
5. Nathan Rosenstein, *Rome at War: Farms, Families, and Death in the Middle Republic* (Chapel Hill: University of North Carolina Press, 2004), 141–69.

6   Plutarch, *Tiberius Gracchus* 8; Appian, *Civil Wars* 1.7. For the question of citizen versus enslaved labor, see Dan-el Padilla Peralta, "Barbarians Inside the Gate, Part II: Immigrant Labor and Its Discontents," *Eidolon*, November 12, 2015, https://eidolon.pub/barbarians-inside-the-gate-part-ii-c22c5becd228. Padilla Peralta provides a compelling argument for understanding the dynamics of Roman enslaved labor as an analogue to immigrant labor in the United States.
7   G. E. M. de Ste. Croix, *The Class Struggle in the Ancient Greek World: From the Archaic Age to the Arab Conquests* (Ithaca, NY: Cornell University Press, 1981), 350–72.
8   Sallust, *Jugurthine War* 8.1.
9   Rakesh Kochhar and Anthony Cilluffo, "How Wealth Inequality Has Changed in the U.S. Since the Great Recession, by Race, Ethnicity and Income," *Pew Research Center*, November 1, 2017, https://www.pewresearch.org/fact-tank/2017/11/01/how-wealth-inequality-has-changed-in-the-u-s-since-the-great-recession-by-race-ethnicity-and-income/; Chuck Collins, "US Billionaire Wealth Surges Past $1 Trillion Since Beginning of Pandemic," *Inequality.org*, November 25, 2020, https://inequality.org/great-divide/u-s-billionaire-wealth-surges-past-1-trillion-since-beginning-of-pandemic/; Christopher Ingraham, "World's Richest Men Added Billions to Their Fortunes Last Year as Others Struggled," *Washington Post*, January 1, 2021, https://www.washingtonpost.com/business/2021/01/01/bezos-musk-wealth-pandemic/.
10 UN Data, "Gini Index (World Bank Estimate)," May 14, 2021, http://data.un.org/Data.aspx?d=WDI&f=Indicator_Code%3ASI.POV.GINI. BBC, "Who, What, Why: What Is the Gini Coefficient?," March 12, 2015, https://www.bbc.com/news/blogs-magazine-monitor-31847943.
11 Pew Research Center, "Most Americans Say There Is Too Much Economic Inequality in the U.S., but Fewer than Half Call It a Top Priority," January 9, 2020, https://www.pewresearch.org/social-trends/2020/01/09/trends-in-income-and-wealth-inequality/.
12 Lawrence Mishel and Jori Kandra, "CEO Compensation Surged 14% in 2019 to $21.3 Million: CEOs Now Earn 320 Times as Much as a Typical Worker," August 18, 2020, https://www.epi.org/publication/ceo-compensation-surged-14-in-2019-to-21-3-million-ceos-now-earn-320-times-as-much-as-a-typical-worker/; Jena McGregor, "Average CEO Earnings Soared to $21.3 Million Last Year and Could Rise Again in 2020 despite the Coronavirus Recession," *Washington Post*, August 18, 2020, https://www.washingtonpost.com/business/2020/08/18/corporate-executive-pay-increase/; Dan Marcec, "Trends to Watch: An Early Look at CEO Pay and the Impact of COVID-19 on Employee Compensation," *Harvard Law School Forum on Corporate Governance*, March 31, 2021, https://corpgov.law.harvard.edu/2021/03/31/trends-to-watch-an-early-look-at-ceo-pay-and-the-impact-of-covid-19-on-employee-compensation/.
13 Bureau of Labor Statistics, "Occupational Employment and Wages, May 2020: 11-1011 Chief Executives," March 31, 2021, https://www.bls.gov/oes/current/oes111011.htm; Glenn Kessler, Salvador Rizzo and Adriana Usero, "Fact-checking Biden's 2021 Address to Congress," *Washington Post*, April 28, 2021, https://www.washingtonpost.com/politics/2021/04/28/fact-checking-bidens-2021-address-congress/.
14 Bureau of Labor Statistics, "Union Members Summary," January 22, 2021, https://www.bls.gov/news.release/union2.nr0.htm.

15 Noam Scheiber, "Middle-Class Pay Lost Pace. Is Washington to Blame?," *New York Times*, May 13, 2021, https://www.nytimes.com/2021/05/13/business/economy/middle-class-pay.html.

16 Todd C. Frankel, "A Majority of the People Arrested for Capitol Riot Had a History of Financial Trouble," *Washington Post*, February 10, 2021, https://www.washingtonpost.com/business/2021/02/10/capitol-insurrectionists-jenna-ryan-financial-problems/.

17 Jonathan O'Connell, Andrew Van Dam, Aaron Gregg and Alyssa Fowers, "More than Half of Emergency Small-Business Funds Went to Larger Businesses, New Data Shows," *Washington Post*, December 2, 2020, https://www.washingtonpost.com/business/2020/12/01/ppp-sba-data/; Sacha Pfeiffer, "Scores of Private Charitable Foundations Got Paycheck Protection Program Money," *NPR: Morning Edition*, December 16, 2020, https://www.npr.org/2020/12/16/946739398/scores-of-private-charitable-foundations-got-paycheck-protection-program-money; Douglas MacMillan, Peter Whoriskey and Jonathan O'Connell, "America's Biggest Companies Are Flourishing during the Pandemic and Putting Thousands of People out of Work," *Washington Post*, December 16, 2020, https://www.washingtonpost.com/graphics/2020/business/50-biggest-companies-coronavirus-layoffs/.

18 For the idea that the Roman people, who once bestowed military commands and public offices, were reduced to hoping for "bread and circuses," see Juvenal *Satires* 10.77–81. For the buying off of the political elite, see Tacitus, *Annals* 1.2. See further, de Ste. Croix, *Class Struggle* 363–64, 372–408.

Chapter 5 Political violence can become normalized

1 Plutarch, *Tiberius Gracchus* 20. For violence in the Roman Republic generally, see Andrew Lintott, *Violence in Republican Rome*, 2nd ed. (Oxford: Oxford University Press, 1999).

2 Plutarch, *Tiberius Gracchus* 20; Appian, *Civil Wars* 1.2, 17; Velleius Paterculus, *Roman History* 2.3.3. Exceptions to this point include the episode of Coriolanus in the 490s BCE (Plutarch, *Coriolanus* 17) and the violence against Verginia by her father and Appius Claudius, the decemvir, in 449 BCE (Livy, *History of Rome* 3.44–50).

3 For Tiberius and Gaius Gracchus generally, in addition to Plutarch's *Lives*, see David L. Stockton, *The Gracchi* (Oxford: Clarendon Press, 1979); Suzanne Dixon, *Cornelia, Mother of the Gracchi* (London: Routledge, 2007).

4 Plutarch, *Tiberius Gracchus* 9; Appian, *Civil Wars* 1.9.

5 Plutarch, *Tiberius Gracchus* 10–11.

6 Levitsky and Ziblatt, *How Democracies Die* 8–9, 128–31, 138.

7 Plutarch, *Tiberius Gracchus* 16–20; Appian, *Civil Wars* 1.14–15.

8 Appian, *Civil Wars* 1.21–27; Plutarch, *Gaius Gracchus* 4–6; Christopher S. Mackay, *Breakdown of the Roman Republic: From Oligarchy to Empire* (Cambridge: Cambridge University Press, 2009), 58–82; Edward J. Watts, *Mortal Republic: How Rome Fell into Tyranny* (New York: Basic Books, 2018), 92–98.

9 Cicero, *On the Orator* 2.132–34; Plutarch, *Gaius Gracchus* 8–9, 13–18; Appian, *Civil Wars* 1.21–27.

10 For the violence of Marius, Cinna, and Sulla, see Sallust, *Histories* 1.48; Appian, *Civil Wars* 1.72–74, 95–96; Plutarch, *Marius* 43–44, *Sulla* 30–31; Velleius Paterculus, *Roman History* 2.28.

11 Alfred L. Brophy, *Reconstructing the Dreamland: The Tulsa Race Riot of 1921, Race Reparations, and Reconciliation* (Oxford: Oxford University Press, 2002).
12 Sidney Lens, *The Labor Wars: From the Molly Maguires to the Sit Downs* (Chicago: Haymarket Books, 2008; originally Garden City, NY: Doubleday, 1973).
13 William C. Blizzard, *When Miners March* (Gay, WV: Appalachian Community Press, 2005); David Corbin, *Gun Thugs, Rednecks, and Radicals: A Documentary History of the West Virginia Mine Wars* (Oakland: PM Press, 2011). It is worth noting that aerial attacks were used at both Tulsa and Blair Mountain, some of the earliest in American history.
14 For these violent attacks, see Adeel Hassan, "White Supremacist Guilty of Killing 2 Who Came to Aid of Black Teens," *New York Times*, February 21, 2020, https://www.nytimes.com/2020/02/21/us/white-supremacist-guilty-of-killing-2-who-came-to-aid-of-black-teens.html; Mitch Smith, "James Fields Sentenced to Life in Prison for Death of Heather Heyer in Charlottesville," *New York Times*, June 28, 2019, https://www.nytimes.com/2019/06/28/us/james-fields-sentencing.html; Julia Carrie Wong, "El Paso Shooting: Suspect Confesses to Targeting Mexicans, Officials Say," *Guardian*, August 9, 2019, https://www.theguardian.com/us-news/2019/aug/09/el-paso-shooting-suspect-confessed-attack-mexicans; Alexis Stevens and Shaddi Abusaid, "'A Crime against Us All.' Outrage, Grief after Deadly Spa Shootings," *Atlanta Journal-Constitution*, March 17, 2021, https://www.ajc.com/news/exclusive-spa-shooting-suspect-bought-gun-hours-before-deadly-spree/FEURWVYBEFBMJP7GLOQ6AQJ27A/; Richard Fausset and Neil Vigdor, "8 People Killed in Atlanta-Area Shootings at Massage Parlors," *New York Times*, March 16, 2021, https://www.nytimes.com/2021/03/16/us/atlanta-shootings-massage-parlor.html.
15 William Cummings, "'Only in the Panhandle:' Trump Chuckles When Audience Member Suggests Shooting Migrants," *USA Today*, May 9, 2019, https://www.usatoday.com/story/news/politics/onpolitics/2019/05/09/trump-chuckles-shooting-migrants/1150160001/; J. M. Reiger, "When a Rallygoer Suggested Shooting Immigrants in May, Trump Made a Joke," *Washington Post*, August 5, 2019, https://www.washingtonpost.com/politics/2019/08/05/when-rally-goer-suggested-shooting-immigrants-may-trump-made-joke/.
16 Karoun Demirjian and Devlin Barrett, "Trump's Pentagon Chief, Attributes Capitol Breach to 'Organized Conspiracy,'" *Washington Post*, May 12, 2021, https://www.washingtonpost.com/national-security/christopher-miller-jeffrey-rosen-capitol-riot/2021/05/11/8eb22bda-b2a5-11eb-ab43-bebddc5a0f65_story.html; Whitney Wild, Jeremy Herb, and Tom Foreman, "New Radio and Video Footage Shows a Coordinated Attack and Officers' Restraint," *CNN*, February 15, 2021, https://www.cnn.com/2021/02/15/politics/video-dispatches-capitol-riots/index.html.

Chapter 6 Strongmen do not save republics

1 Plutarch, *Marius*, 4; for Marius on this point and generally, see Federico Santangelo, *Marius* (London: Bloomsbury, 2016), 18–20.
2 For this war, see Sallust, *The Jugurthine War*.
3 Sallust, *Jugurthine War* 64–65, 84; Plutarch, *Marius* 8–9.
4 Sallust, *Jugurthine War* 84–87.
5 For Marius's victories and military reforms, see Sallust, *Jugurthine War* 87–113; Plutarch, *Marius* 10–13; Santangelo, *Marius* 25–41.
6 Cicero, *Pro Sestio* 37–38; Plutarch, *Marius* 27.

7   For Marius and Saturninus, see Sallust, *Jugurthine War* 86, 113–14; Plutarch, *Marius* 28–31; Appian, *Civil Wars* 1.28–33; Santangelo, *Marius* 57–65; Ernst Badian, "The Death of Saturninus," *Chiron* 14 (1984): 101–47.
8   For these events, see Plutarch, *Marius* 34–45, *Sulla* 7–10; Appian, *Civil Wars* 1.55–75; Santangelo, *Marius* 74–94.
9   Ruth Ben-Ghiat, *Strongmen: Mussolini to the Present* (New York: W.W Norton, 2020).
10 Richard D. White, *Kingfish: The Reign of Huey P. Long* (New York: Random House, 2006); Richard C. Cortner, *The Kingfish and the Constitution: Huey Long, the First Amendment, and the Emergence of Modern Press Freedom in America* (Westport, CT: Greenwood Press, 1996); John A. Farrell, *Richard Nixon: The Life* (New York: Doubleday, 2017); Richard Perlstein, *Nixonland: The Rise of a President and the Fracturing of America* (New York: Scribner, 2008).
11 David A. Bell, "Methods of Power: How Do Authoritarians Rule?," *Nation*, April 6, 2021, https://www.thenation.com/article/society/ruth-ben-ghiat-strongmen/.
12 Jeremy Diamond, "Trump: I Could 'Shoot Somebody and I Wouldn't Lose Voters,'" *CNN*, January 24, 2016, https://www.cnn.com/2016/01/23/politics/donald-trump-shoot-somebody-support/index.html.
13 Jack Healy, "These Are the 5 People Who Died in the Capitol Riot," *New York Times*, January 11, 2021, https://www.nytimes.com/2021/01/11/us/who-died-in-capitol-building-attack.html; Peter Hermann, "Two Officers Who Helped Fight the Capitol Mob Died by Suicide. Many More Are Hurting," *Washington Post*, February 12, 2021, https://www.washingtonpost.com/local/public-safety/police-officer-suicides-capitol-riot/2021/02/11/94804ee2-665c-11eb-886d-5264d4ceb46d_story.html.
14 Steve Peoples, "Trump Remains Dominant Force in GOP Following Acquittal," *Associated Press*, February 14, 2021, https://apnews.com/article/donald-trump-capitol-siege-impeachments-acquittals-54a562159db21bd2c806c0c3c366be62; Lisa Lerer, "Marooned at Mar-a-Lago, Trump Still Has Iron Grip on Republicans," *New York Times*, May 8, 2021, https://www.nytimes.com/2021/05/08/us/politics/trump-republicans-liz-cheney.html.
15 Sallust ends his *Jugurthine War* (114) with the statement that the hope and the resources of the state (*civitas*) resided in Marius alone, an ominous statement in a republic.
16 Donald J. Trump, "Address Accepting the Presidential Nomination at the Republican National Convention in Cleveland, Ohio," *The American Presidency Project*, July 21, 2016, https://www.presidency.ucsb.edu/documents/address-accepting-the-presidential-nomination-the-republican-national-convention-cleveland.
17 President Donald Trump, "Statement by the President," June 1, 2020. Available at https://www.whitehouse.gov/briefings-statements/statement-by-the-president-39/.
18 Domenico Mantenaro, "What Is the Insurrection Act That Trump Is Threatening to Invoke?," *NPR*, June 1, 2020, https://www.npr.org/2020/06/01/867467714/what-is-the-insurrection-act-that-trump-is-threatening-to-invoke; Katie Rogers, Jonathan Martin, and Maggie Haberman, "As Trump Calls Protesters 'Terrorists,' Tear Gas Clears a Path for His Walk to a Church," *New York Times* June 1, 2020, https://www.nytimes.com/2020/06/01/us/politics/trump-governors.html; Alex Horton, "Use of Medical Helicopter to Target Protesters Is under Investigation, National Guard Says," *Washington Post*, June 2, 2020, https://www.washingtonpost.com/national-security/2020/06/02/helicopter-protest-dc/; Katie Shepherd, "North Carolina GOP Lawmaker Urges Trump to Suspend Civil Liberties to Keep Power: 'Invoke the Insurrection Act,'" *Washington Post*, December 16, 2020, https://www.washingtonpost.com/nation/2020/12/16/north-carolina-republican-trump-insurrection/.

NOTES   105

   For a particularly strong statement advocating invocation of the Insurrection Act, see Senator Tom Cotton's op-ed "Send in the Troops," *New York Times*, June 3, 2020, https://www.nytimes.com/2020/06/03/opinion/tom-cotton-protests-military.html.
19 Jeffrey Goldberg, "James Mattis Denounces President Trump, Describes Him as a Threat to the Constitution," *Atlantic* June 3, 2020, https://www.theatlantic.com/politics/archive/2020/06/james-mattis-denounces-trump-protests-militarization/612640/; Thomas Gibbons-Neff, Helene Cooper, Eric Schmitt, and Jennifer Steinhauer, "Former Commanders Fault Trump's Use of Troops against Protesters," *New York Times*, June 3, 2020, https://www.nytimes.com/2020/06/02/us/politics/military-national-guard-trump-protests.html; Jon Bateman, "The Guardrails Are off the U.S. Military," *Politico*, June 6, 2020, https://www.politico.com/news/magazine/2020/06/06/the-guardrails-are-off-the-us-military-303959.
20 Jeffrey Goldberg, "Trump: Americans Who Died in War Are 'Losers' and 'Suckers,'" *Atlantic*, September 3, 2020, https://www.theatlantic.com/politics/archive/2020/09/trump-americans-who-died-at-war-are-losers-and-suckers/615997/; Open Letter from Senior Military Leaders, https://cdn.donaldjtrump.com/public-files/press_assets/235-military-leaders-endorse-president-trump-final.pdf; Richard Sisk, "Dozens of Retired Generals, Admirals Sign Letter Backing Trump for Reelection," *Military.com*, September 15, 2020, https://www.military.com/daily-news/2020/09/15/dozens-of-retired-generals-admirals-sign-letter-backing-trump-reelection.html.
21 Flag Officers 4 America, "Open Letter from Retired Generals and Admirals," May 10, 2021, https://flagofficers4america.com/opening-statement#393e50a9-590e-4cf3-a356-84bf2eec4e5b; Bryan Bender, "'Disturbing and Reckless': Retired Brass Spread Election Lie in Attack on Biden, Democrats," *Politico*, May 11, 2021, https://www.politico.com/news/2021/05/11/retired-brass-biden-election-487374.

Chapter 7 The rights and responsibilities of citizenship need to be shared and extended

1 Livy, *History of Rome* 1.1–16. It should also be noted that Romulus kills Remus, his twin brother in a dispute, thus marking the origins of Roman civil strife.
2 Ramsay MacMullen, *Enemies of the Roman Order: Treason, Unrest, and Alienation in the Empire* (London: Routledge, 1992), 46–94, 128–162; David Noy, *Foreigners at Rome: Citizens and Strangers* (London: Duckworth, 2000), 37–47.
3 Lucia Cecchet and Anna Busett, eds. *Citizens in the Graeco-Roman World: Aspects of Citizenship from the Archaic Period to AD 212* (Leiden; Boston: Brill, 2017); Barry Strauss, "Why Ancient Rome Needed Immigrants to Become Powerful," *History*, April 3, 2019, https://www.history.com/news/ancient-rome-immigration-slavery#:~:text=As%20the%20Roman%20emperors%20sought,had%20to%20have%20new%20blood.; Mary Beard, "Ancient Rome and Today's Migrant Crisis," *Wall Street Journal*, October 16, 2015, https://www.wsj.com/articles/ancient-rome-and-todays-migrant-crisis-1445005978; A.N. Sherwin-White, *The Roman Citizenship*, 2nd ed. (Oxford: Clarendon Press, 1973).
4 Appian, *Civil Wars* 1.34.
5 Velleius Paterculus, *Roman History* 2.14; Appian, *Civil Wars* 1.35–38.

6   Dan-el Padilla Peralta, "Barbarians Inside the Gate, Part I: Fears of Immigration in Ancient Rome and Today," *Eidolon*, November 9, 2015, https://eidolon.pub/barbarians-inside-the-gate-part-i-c175057b340f.
7   Appian, *Civil Wars* 1.35–49.
8   Cicero, *Pro Flacco* 60; Livy, *Periochae* 78; Valerius Maximus, *Memorable Deeds and Sayings* 9.2.3–4; Plutarch, *Sulla* 24.4; Appian, *Mithridatic Wars* 22–23.
9   Bridgett A. King, ed., *Voting Rights in America: Primary Documents in Context* (Santa Barbara, CA: ABC-CLIO, 2020). For a timeline of voting restrictions and expansions, see Pence Law Library Guides, "The Fight for the Right to Vote," October 2, 2020, https://wcl.american.libguides.com/voting/history/timeline.
10 Nick Corasaniti and Reid J. Epstein, "What Georgia's Voting Law Really Does," *New York Times*, April 2, 2021, https://www.nytimes.com/2021/04/02/us/politics/georgia-voting-law-annotated.html; Nick Corasaniti and Reid J. Epstein, "Florida and Texas Join the March to Restrict Voting Access," *New York Times*, May 6, 2021, https://www.nytimes.com/2021/05/06/us/politics/florida-texas-voting-rights-bills.html.
11 Padilla Peralta, "Barbarians Inside the Gate, Part II."
12 Reid Epstein, "NCLR Head: Obama 'Deporter-in-Chief,'" *Politico*, March 4, 2014, https://www.politico.com/story/2014/03/national-council-of-la-raza-janet-murguia-barack-obama-deporter-in-chief-immigration-104217; Jean Guerrero, "3 Million People Were Deported under Obama. What Will Biden Do about It?," *New York Times*, January 23, 2021, https://www.nytimes.com/2021/01/23/opinion/sunday/immigration-reform-biden.html.
13 Time Staff, "Donald Trump's Presidential Announcement Speech," *Time*, June 16, 2015, https://time.com/3923128/donald-trump-announcement-speech/.
14 Aline Barros, "US Court Clears Path for Fast-Track Citizenship for Foreign-Born Military Service Members," *Voice of America News*, September 3, 2020, https://www.voanews.com/usa/immigration/us-court-clears-path-fast-track-citizenship-foreign-born-military-service-members.
15 For the contentious debate over what to call US detention centers, see Masha Gessen, "The Unimaginable Reality of American Concentration Camps." *New Yorker*, June 21, 2019, https://www.newyorker.com/news/our-columnists/the-unimaginable-reality-of-american-concentration-camps; Jack Holmes, "An Expert on Concentration Camps Says That's Exactly What the U.S. Is Running at the Border," *Esquire*, June 13, 2019, https://www.esquire.com/news-politics/a27813648/concentration-camps-southern-border-migrant-detention-facilities-trump/.
16 Miriam Jordan, "Migrants Separated from Their Children Will Be Allowed into U.S.," *New York Times*, May 3, 2021, https://www.nytimes.com/2021/05/03/us/migrant-family-separation.html; Rick Jervis, "Biden's Effort to Reunite Trump-Era Separated Families Is Trickiest Immigration Challenge," *USA Today*, January 24, 2021, https://www.usatoday.com/story/news/nation/2021/01/23/family-separations-trump-biden-administration-immigration-rules/6672057002/.
17 Arelis R. Hernández and Nick Miroff, "Facing Coronavirus Pandemic, Trump Suspends Immigration Laws and Showcases Vision for Locked-down Border," *Washington Post* April 3, 2020, https://www.washingtonpost.com/national/coronavirus-trump-immigration-border/2020/04/03/23cb025a-74f9-11ea-ae50-7148009252e3_story.html.

For how Trump continued to exploit the pandemic to restrict immigration, see Zolan Kanno-Youngs and Maggie Haberman, "Trump Administration Moves to Solidify Restrictive Immigration Policies," *New York Times*, August 26, 2020, https://www.nytimes.com/2020/06/12/us/politics/coronavirus-trump-immigration-policies.html.

18 For these cases, see Paige St. John and Joel Rubin, "ICE Held an American Man in Custody for 1,273 Days. He's Not the Only One Who Had to Prove His Citizenship," *Los Angeles Times* April 27, 2018, https://www.latimes.com/local/lanow/la-me-citizens-ice-20180427-htmlstory.html; Obed Manuel, "Francisco Galicia, Dallas-born Teen Held by Border Patrol, ICE, Gets His U.S. Passport," *Dallas Morning News*, December 20, 2019, https://www.dallasnews.com/news/immigration/2019/12/20/francisco-galicia-dallas-born-teen-held-by-border-patrol-ice-receives-us-passport/.

19 Tom McCarthy, "Trump Rally Crowd Chants 'Send Her Back' after President Attacks Ilhan Omar," *Guardian*, July 18, 2019, https://www.theguardian.com/us-news/2019/jul/17/trump-rally-send-her-back-ilhan-omar.

20 See, among many possible examples, Pia Orrenius, "Benefits of Immigration Outweigh the Costs," *Catalyst: A Journal of Ideas from the Bush Institute*, Spring 2016, available at https://www.bushcenter.org/catalyst/north-american-century/benefits-of-immigration-outweigh-costs.html; John Cassidy, "Why the United States Needs More Immigrants," *New Yorker*, June 22, 2018. https://www.newyorker.com/news/our-columnists/why-the-united-states-needs-more-immigrants.

21 Alfredo Corchado and Todd J. Gillman, "In South Texas, Trump Says His Border Wall Saves Lives and Jobs, and Warns of Danger from Biden's Looser Policies," *Dallas Morning News*, January 12, 2021, https://www.dallasnews.com/news/politics/2021/01/12/trump-heads-to-south-texas-for-victory-lap-at-border-wall/. For Trump's remarks, see Donald J. Trump, "Remarks by President Trump at the 45th Mile of New Border Wall - Reynosa-McAllen, TX," https://www.whitehouse.gov/briefings-statements/remarks-president-trump-45th-mile-new-border-wall-reynosa-mcallen-tx/. For Biden's executive order, see Nick Miroff and Arelis R. Hernández, "Biden Orders a 'Pause' on Border Wall Construction, Bringing Crews to Halt," *Washington Post*, January 20, 2021, https://www.washingtonpost.com/national/biden-border-wall-executive-order/2021/01/20/5f472456-5b32-11eb-aaad-93988621dd28_story.html.

22 Maria Sacchetti, "Biden Administration to Pause Deportations, Curtail Arrests," *Washington Post*, January 21, 2021, https://www.washingtonpost.com/immigration/biden-administration-to-pause-deportations-curtail-arrests/2021/01/21/73a0682c-5ba0-11eb-b8bd-ee36b1cd18bf_story.html.

23 The White House, "Statement by President Joe Biden on Refugee Admissions," May 3, 2021, https://www.whitehouse.gov/briefing-room/statements-releases/2021/05/03/statement-by-president-joe-biden-on-refugee-admissions/; Editorial Board, "Biden Promised to Rebuild Refugee Admissions. He's on Course to Decimate Them," *Washington Post*, April 14, 2021, https://www.washingtonpost.com/opinions/biden-promised-to-rebuild-refugee-admissions-hes-on-course-to-decimate-them/2021/04/14/cf8cc8a4-9bda-11eb-9d05-ae06f4529ece_story.html.

Chapter 8 Civic virtue is as important as the constitution and laws

1. For the office of dictator, see Mark B. Wilson, *Dictator: The Evolution of the Roman Dictatorship* (Ann Arbor: University of Michigan Press, 2021).
2. Livy, *History of Rome* 3.26–30.
3. Livy, *History of Rome* 3.26.7.
4. Plutarch, *Sulla* 27–29; Appian, *Civil Wars* 1.76–94; Velleius Paterculus, *Roman History* 2.24–28; Ernst Badian, "Waiting for Sulla," in *Studies in Greek and Roman History* (New York: Barnes and Noble, 1964), 206–34; Arthur Keaveney, *Sulla: The Last Republican*, 2nd ed. (London: Routledge, 2005), 117–202.
5. Sallust, *Histories* 1.48; Plutarch, *Sulla* 30-31; Appian, *Civil Wars* 1.95–96.
6. Appian, *Civil Wars* 1.101.
7. Gary Wills, *Cincinnatus: George Washington and the Enlightenment* (Garden City: Doubleday, 1984); Rob Hardy, "Cincinnatus," *Washington Library: Digital Encyclopedia*, https://www.mountvernon.org/library/digitalhistory/digital-encyclopedia/article/cincinnatus.
8. Dan Barry and Sheera Frenkel, "'Be There. Will Be Wild!': Trump All but Circled the Date," *New York Times*, January 8, 2021, https://www.nytimes.com/2021/01/06/us/politics/capitol-mob-trump-supporters.html.
9. Maggie Haberman, "Trump Told Crowd, 'You Will Never Take Back Our Country with Weakness,'" *New York Times*, January 6, 2021, https://www.nytimes.com/2021/01/06/us/politics/trump-speech-capitol.html; Aaron Blake, "What Trump Said before His Supporters Stormed the Capitol, Annotated," *Washington Post*, January 11, 2021, https://www.washingtonpost.com/politics/interactive/2021/annotated-trump-speech-jan-6-capitol/.
10. Zeynep Tufekci, "'This Must Be Your First,' Acting as if Trump Is Trying to Stage a Coup Is the Best Way to Ensure He Won't," *Atlantic*, December 7, 2020, https://www.theatlantic.com/ideas/archive/2020/12/trumps-farcical-inept-and-deadly-serious-coup-attempt/617309/; Eugene Robinson, "We Just Saw an Attempted Coup d'etat. Blame Trump. Blame His Republican Enablers," *Washington Post*, January 6, 2021, https://www.washingtonpost.com/opinions/trump-has-wounded-this-country-it-will-take-a-long-long-time-for-us-to-heal/2021/01/06/c9f74102-5068-11eb-bda4-615aaefd0555_story.html; Naunihal Singh, "Was the U.S. Capitol Riot Really a Coup? Here's Why Definitions Matter," *Washington Post*, January 9, 2021, https://www.washingtonpost.com/politics/2021/01/09/was-us-capitol-riot-really-coup-heres-why-definitions-matter/; Timothy Snyder, "The American Abyss," *New York Times Magazine*, January 9, 2021, https://www.nytimes.com/2021/01/09/magazine/trump-coup.html.
11. For the storming of the Capitol, see Rachel Weiner and Spencer S. Hsu, "Armed 'Quick Reaction Force' Was Waiting for Order to Storm Capitol, DOJ Says," *Washington Post*, April 14, 2021, https://www.washingtonpost.com/local/legal-issues/quick-reaction-force-capitol-riot/2021/04/14/2021da66-9d39-11eb-8005-bffc3a39f6d3_story.html; Mark Mazzetti, Helene Cooper, Jennifer Steinhauer, Zolan Kanno-Youngs, and Luke Broadwater, "Inside a Deadly Siege: How a String of Failures Led to a Dark Day at the Capitol," *New York Times*, January 11, 2021, https://www.nytimes.com/2021/01/10/us/politics/capitol-siege-security.html; George Petras, Janet Loehrke, Roman Padilla, Javie Zarracina, and Jennifer Borresen, "Timeline: How a Trump Mob Stormed the US Capitol, Forcing Washington into Lockdown," *USA*

Today, January 8, 2021, https://www.usatoday.com/web-stories/timeline-how-a-trump-mob-stormed-the-us-capitol-forcing-washington-into-lockdown/.

12 Karen Yourish, Larry Buchanan, and Denise Lu, "The 147 Republicans Who Voted to Overturn Election Results," *New York Times*, January 7, 2021, https://www.nytimes.com/interactive/2021/01/07/us/elections/electoral-college-biden-objectors.html.

13 For the vote to confirm Biden's election, see Rosalind S. Helderman, Karoun Demirjian, Seung Min Kim, and Mike DeBonis, "Congress Affirms Biden's Presidential Win Following Riot at U.S. Capitol," *Washington Post*, January 7, 2021, https://www.washingtonpost.com/politics/congress-resumes-work-to-confirm-biden-win-on-historic-day-marred-by-riot/2021/01/06/4c3729dc-5039-11eb-b96e-0e54447b23a1_story.html.

14 John Wagner, "McCarthy Announces Opposition to Commission to Investigate Deadly Jan. 6 Attack on Capitol by Pro-Trump Mob," *Washington Post*, May 18, 2021, https://www.washingtonpost.com/powerpost/mccarthy-oppose-commission-capitol-attack/2021/05/18/7579c386-b7e0-11eb-a6b1-81296da0339b_story.html; Mike DeBonis, "McConnell Comes out against Jan. 6 Commission, Imperiling Its Chances of Becoming Law," *Washington Post*, May 19, 2021, https://www.washingtonpost.com/politics/mcconnell-comes-out-against-jan-6-commission-imperiling-its-chances-of-becoming-law/2021/05/19/60de1f52-b8b3-11eb-a5fe-bb49dc89a248_story.html.

15 Molly Beck, "Ron Johnson Says Capitol Attackers 'Love This Country' but He Would Have Felt Unsafe If Black Lives Matter Stormed Building Instead," *Milwaukee Journal Sentinel*, March 12, 2021, https://www.jsonline.com/story/news/politics/2021/03/12/wisconsin-senator-ron-johnson-comment-capitol-black-lives-matter-called-racist/4674016001/.

16 Colby Itkowitz, "Senate Votes to Award Officer Eugene Goodman the Congressional Gold Medal," *Washington Post*, February 12, 2021, https://www.washingtonpost.com/politics/capitol-riot-goodman-impeachment/2021/02/12/ae9f074e-6d89-11eb-9f80-3d7646ce1bc0_story.html.

17 The New York Times, "Trump's Capitol Tweets Deleted, Account Now Locked for 12 Hours," *New York Times*, January 6, 2021, https://www.nytimes.com/2021/01/06/us/politics/twitter-deletes-trump-tweet.html. Twitter permanently deleted Trump's account on January 8, 2021; see Twitter Inc., "Permanent Suspension of @realDonaldTrump," January 8, 2021, https://blog.twitter.com/en_us/topics/company/2020/suspension.html.

18 Sam Levine and Lauren Gambino, "Donald Trump Acquitted in Second Impeachment Trial," *Guardian*, February 13, 2021, https://www.theguardian.com/us-news/2021/feb/13/donald-trump-acquitted-impeachment-trial; Tucker Higgins, "GOP Senators Who Voted to Convict Trump Are Now Facing Backlash in Their Home States," *CNBC*, February 14, 2021, https://www.cnbc.com/2021/02/14/gop-senators-who-voted-to-impeach-trump-facing-heat-at-home.html.

19 Catie Edmondson and Nicholas Fandos, "Republicans Oust Defiant Cheney, Confirming Trump's Grasp on the Party," *New York Times*, May 12, 2021, https://www.nytimes.com/2021/05/12/us/politics/liz-cheney-trump-republicans.html; Liz Cheney, "The GOP Is at a Turning Point. History Is Watching Us," *Washington Post*, May 5, 2021, https://www.washingtonpost.com/opinions/2021/05/05/liz-cheney-republican-party-turning-point/.

20 Tom Jackman and Spencer S. Hsu, "Hundreds of People Stormed the Capitol. Most Won't Face Hefty Prison Terms, Legal Experts Say," *Washington Post*, May 13, 2021, https://www.washingtonpost.com/nation/2021/05/13/capitol-rioters-sentencing/; Rachel Axon, Dinah Pulver, Rachel Stassen-Berger, Jayme Fraser, Josh Salman, Nicholas Penzenstadler, Katie Wedell, Morgan Hines, and David Baratz, "Capitol Riot Arrests: See Who's Been Charged across the U.S.," *USA Today*, October 14, 2021, https://www.usatoday.com/storytelling/capitol-riot-mob-arrests/.

21 Brittany Shammas, "A GOP Congressman Compared Capitol Rioters to Tourists. Photos Show Him Barricading a Door," *Washington Post*, May 18, 2021, https://www.washingtonpost.com/politics/2021/05/18/clyde-tourist-capitol-riot-photos/; Colby Itkowitz, "'Normal Tourist Visit': Republicans Recast Deadly Jan. 6 Attack by Pro-Trump Mob," *Washington Post*, May 12, 2021, https://www.washingtonpost.com/politics/trump-riot-capitol-republicans/2021/05/12/dcc03342-b351-11eb-a980-a60af976ed44_story.html.

Chapter 9 A reckoning with the oppressed cannot be denied

1 For these rebellions in Sicily, see Diodorus Siculus, *The Library of History* 34/35.2.1–48, 36.1–11; Florus, *Epitome of Roman History* 2.7.1–12; Brent D. Shaw, *Spartacus and the Slave Wars: A Brief History with Documents* (Boston: Bedford, 2018).

2 For Roman slavery in general, see Page DuBois, *Slavery: Antiquity and Its Legacy* (Oxford: Oxford University Press, 2009); Sandra R. Joshel, *Slavery in the Roman World* (Cambridge: Cambridge University Press, 2010). For slavery in general, see Orlando Patterson, *Slavery and Social Death: A Comparative Study* (Cambridge, MA: Harvard University Press, 2018).

3 For this point, see Nell Irving Painter, *The History of White People* (New York: W.W. Norton, 2010), 1–33.

4 For ancient sources that address this point, see most importantly Aristotle, *Politics* 1.5–6; Seneca, *Moral Epistles* 47; Justinian, *Institutes* 1.3. For a critique of Seneca and the "good slave master," see Stephanie McCarter, "Seneca's 'Lost Cause': the Myth of the Noble Stoic/Southerner Slave Owner," *Eidolon*, February 1, 2019, https://eidolon.pub/senecas-lost-cause-cfcbb5d15d32.

5 For Tacitus's account of these events, see *Annals* 13.32.1, 14.42–45.

6 For Spartacus, see Plutarch, *Crassus* 8–11; Appian, *Civil Wars* 1.111–21; Mackay, *Breakdown of the Roman Republic* 203-5; Watts, *Mortal Republic* 151–52, 162–64; Barry Strauss, *The Spartacus War* (New York: Simon & Schuster, 2009).

7 St. Gregory of Nyssa (335–395 CE) provides the rare example. In his *Homilies on Ecclesiastes* (4.335–336), Gregory attacks the practice of slavery and its basis in Christian scripture.

8 For the conviction exception, see, Ava DuVernay, *13th* (Sherman Oaks, CA: Kandoo Films, 2016).

9 For Jim Crow and mass incarceration, see James H. Cone, *The Cross and the Lynching Tree* (Maryknoll, NY: Orbis Books, 2011); Alexander, *The New Jim Crow*; Kendi, *Stamped from the Beginning*; Henry Louis Gates, Jr., *Stony the Road: Reconstruction, White Supremacy, and the Rise of Jim Crow* (New York: Penguin Press, 2019).

10 See the seminal essay reviving the debate on reparations by Ta-Nehisi Coates, "The Case for Reparations," *Atlantic*, June 2014, https://www.theatlantic.com/magazine/archive/2014/06/the-case-for-reparations/361631/. For books that effectively

address the ongoing problem of racism in America, see Ta-Nehisi Coates, *Between the World and Me* (New York: One World, 2015); Ibram X. Kendi, *How to Be an Antiracist* (New York: One World, 2019); Robin DiAngelo, *White Fragility: Why It's so Hard for White People to Talk about Racism* (Boston: Beacon Press, 2018).

11 Carla K. Johnson, Angeliki Kastanis, and Kat Stafford, "Racial Disparities Seen in US Vaccination Drive," *Associated Press*, January 30, 2021, https://apnews.com/article/race-and-ethnicity-health-coronavirus-pandemic-hispanics-d0746b028cf56231dbcdeda0fba24314.

12 Rev. Bryan N. Massingale, "The Racist Attack on Our Nation's Capitol," *America Magazine*, January 6, 2021 https://www.americamagazine.org/politics-society/2021/01/06/us-capitol-trump-riot-racist-239662.

13 Neil Bhutta, Andrew C. Chang, Lisa J. Dettling, and Joanne W. Hsu with assistance from Julia Hewitt, "Disparities in Wealth by Race and Ethnicity in the 2019 Survey of Consumer Finances," *FEDS Notes*, September 28, 2020, https://www.federalreserve.gov/econres/notes/feds-notes/disparities-in-wealth-by-race-and-ethnicity-in-the-2019-survey-of-consumer-finances-20200928.htm.

14 Seneca, *Moral Epistles* 107.11, *ducunt volentem fata, nolentem trahunt.*

Chapter 10 Elections only work when everyone is willing to lose

1 Asconius, *Commentary on Cicero's In Toga Candida* 75; Plutarch, *Sulla* 32, *Cicero* 10; Barbara Levick, *Catiline* (London: Bloomsbury Academic, 2015), 23–24.

2 Cicero, *Pro Murena* 52; Sallust, *Catiline's War* 26; Plutarch, *Cicero* 14; Dio, *Roman History* 37.29.4.

3 Cicero, *First Catilinarian*. Cicero's four speeches, *The Catilinarians*, are some of his most famous orations.

4 Cicero, *Pro Sestio* 121, *Against Piso* 6; Velleius Paterculus, *Roman History* 2.35.4; Plutarch, *Cicero* 22–23; Appian, *Civil Wars* 2.6–7. For this episode and Cato generally, see Fred Drogula, *Cato the Younger: Life and Death at the End of the Roman Republic* (Oxford: Oxford University Press, 2019), 69–70, 78–79, 89–90.

5 Sabrina Siddiqui, "Mueller's Testimony on Trump and Russia: The Biggest Takeaways," *Guardian*, July 24, 2019, https://www.theguardian.com/us-news/2019/jul/24/robert-mueller-testimony-key-takeaways-exoneration-indictment. For a good and succinct overview of Russian interference in American politics, see Timothy Snyder, *The Road to Unfreedom: Russia, Europe, America* (New York: Tim Duggan Books, 2018), 217–78.

6 Anthony Zurcher, "Donald Trump Suggests Delay to 2020 US Presidential Election," *BBC* July 30, 2020, https://www.bbc.com/news/world-us-canada-53597975.

7 David Smith, "Donald Trump Hints at Assassination of Hillary Clinton by Gun Rights Supporters," *Guardian*, August 10, 2016, https://www.theguardian.com/us-news/2016/aug/09/trump-gun-owners-clinton-judges-second-amendment.

8 Eugene Scott, "Donald Trump on Brokered Convention: 'I Think You'd Have Riots,'" *CNN*, March 17, 2016, https://www.cnn.com/2016/03/16/politics/donald-trump-ted-cruz-brokered-convention/index.html.

9 Morgan Chalfant, "After Senate Acquittal, Trump Tweets Video Showing Him Running for President Indefinitely," *Hill*, February 5, 2020, https://thehill.com/homenews/administration/481728-after-senate-acquittal-trump-tweets-video-showing-him-running-for.

10 Jessica Campisi, "Graham Jokes after Democratic Debate: Third Term for Trump 'Looking Better and Better,'" *Hill,* June 27, 2019, https://thehill.com/blogs/blog-briefing-room/news/450705-graham-jokes-after-democratic-debate-third-term-for-trump.

11 Stephanie Saul, "Lindsey Graham's Long-Shot Mission to Unravel the Election Results," *New York Times,* November 17, 2020, https://www.nytimes.com/2020/11/17/us/politics/lindsey-graham-georgia-trump-biden.html; Amy Gardner, Tom Hamburger, and Josh Dawsey, "Graham's Post-election Call with Raffensperger Will Be Scrutinized in Georgia Probe, Person Familiar with Inquiry Says," *Washington Post,* February 12, 2021, https://www.washingtonpost.com/politics/lindsey-graham-georgia-investigation/2021/02/12/f12faa82-6d6b-11eb-9f80-3d7646ce1bc0_story.html.

12 For these quotations, see Michael Brice-Saddler, "While Bemoaning Mueller Probe, Trump Falsely Says the Constitution Gives Him 'the Right to Do Whatever I Want,'" *Washington Post,* July 23, 2019, https://www.washingtonpost.com/politics/2019/07/23/trump-falsely-tells-auditorium-full-teens-constitution-gives-him-right-do-whatever-i-want/; Brett Samuels and Jordain Carney, "Dershowitz: If President Does Something to Win Election, It's OK unless It's Illegal," *Hill,* January 29, 2020, https://thehill.com/homenews/administration/480566-dershowitz-if-president-does-something-to-win-election-its-ok-unless; Meagan Flynn and Allyson Chiu, "Trump Says His 'Authority Is Total.' Constitutional Experts Have 'No Idea' Where He Got That," *Washington Post,* April 14, 2020, https://www.washingtonpost.com/nation/2020/04/14/trump-power-constitution-coronavirus/.

13 Amy Gardner and Paulina Firozi, "Here's the Full Transcript and Audio of the Call between Trump and Raffensperger," *Washington Post,* January 5, 2021, https://www.washingtonpost.com/politics/trump-raffensperger-call-transcript-georgia-vote/2021/01/03/2768e0cc-4ddd-11eb-83e3-322644d82356_story.html; Amy Gardner, "'I Just Want to Find 11,780 Votes': In Extraordinary Hour-long Call, Trump Pressures Georgia Secretary of State to Recalculate the Vote in His Favor," *Washington Post,* January 3, 2021, https://www.washingtonpost.com/2021/01/03/d45acb92-4dc4-11eb-bda4-615aaefd0555_story.html?arc404=true.

14 Jim Rutenberg, Jo Becker, Eric Lipton, Maggie Haberman, Jonathan Martin, Matthew Rosenberg, and Michael S. Schmidt, "77 Days: Trump's Campaign to Subvert the Election," *New York Times,* January 31, 2021, https://www.nytimes.com/2021/01/31/us/trump-election-lie.html.

15 Rosalind S. Helderman, "Observers Report Ballots and Laptop Computers Have Been Left Unattended in Arizona Recount, according to Secretary of State," *Washington Post,* May 5, 2021, https://www.washingtonpost.com/politics/arizona-recount-observers/2021/05/05/b807c990-adc3-11eb-b476-c3b287e52a01_story.html; Michael Wines, "Arizona Vote Review Is 'Political Theater' and 'Sham,' G.O.P. Leaders Say," *New York Times,* May 17, 2021, https://www.nytimes.com/2021/05/17/us/arizona-audit-trump.html; Amy Gardner, "In Echo of Arizona, Georgia State Judge Orders Fulton County to Allow Local Voters to Inspect Mailed Ballots Cast Last Fall," *Washington Post,* May 21, 2021, https://www.washingtonpost.com/politics/georgia-ballot-inspection/2021/05/21/1e8ad1cc-ba61-11eb-a6b1-81296da0339b_story.html.

16 Michael Gerson, "The Threat of Violence Now Infuses GOP Politics. We Should All Be Afraid," *Washington Post,* May 20, 2021, https://www.washingtonpost.com/opinions/2021/05/20/trump-republicans-violent-threats-election-2024/; Nora

McGreevy, "Was the Capitol Attack Part of a New Wave of Terrorism?," *JSTOR Daily*, February 16, 2021, https://daily.jstor.org/was-the-capitol-attack-part-of-a-new-wave-of-terrorism/; Paul Waldman, "Right-wing Violence Will Now Be a Regular Feature of American Politics," *Washington Post*, January 12, 2021, https://www.washingtonpost.com/opinions/2021/01/12/right-wing-violence-will-now-be-regular-feature-american-politics/.

Chapter 11 Disregard for the civil liberties of some erodes the legal rights of all citizens

1 Sallust, *Catiline's War* 50–55.
2 Cicero, *Letters to His Friends* 5.2, *Against Piso* 6–7; Asconius, *Commentary on Cicero's Against Piso* 6; Levick, *Catiline* 87–107.
3 Cicero, *Letters to Atticus* Book 3, *Letters to Quintus* 1.3, 1.4, *Letters to Friends* 14.1–4; Plutarch, *Cicero* 30–33; Appian, *Civil Wars* 2.15–16; Dio, *Roman History* 38.9–30; Elizabeth Rawson, *Cicero: A Portrait*, (London: Lane Allen, 1975), 112–82.
4 For competing views of the USA PATRIOT Act, see Department of Defense, "Dispelling Some of the Major Myths about the USA PATRIOT Act," https://www.justice.gov/archive/ll/subs/u_myths.htm; American Civil Liberties Union, "Myths and Realities About the Patriot Act," available at https://www.aclu.org/other/myths-and-realities-about-patriot-act, and "How the USA PATRIOT Act Redefines 'Domestic Terrorism,'" https://www.aclu.org/other/how-usa-patriot-act-redefines-domestic-terrorism.
5 For these cases, see Scott Shane, "The Lessons of Anwar al-Awlaki," *New York Times Magazine*, August 27, 2015, https://www.nytimes.com/2015/08/30/magazine/the-lessons-of-anwar-al-awlaki.html; Conor Friedersdorf, "How Team Obama Justifies the Killing of a 16-Year-Old American," *Atlantic*, October 24, 2012, https://www.theatlantic.com/politics/archive/2012/10/how-team-obama-justifies-the-killing-of-a-16-year-old-american/264028/; Glenn Greenwald, "Obama Killed a 16-Year-Old American in Yemen. Trump Just Killed His 8-Year-Old Sister," *Intercept*, January 30, 2017, https://theintercept.com/2017/01/30/obama-killed-a-16-year-old-american-in-yemen-trump-just-killed-his-8-year-old-sister/.
6 Mark Bray, "Five Myths about Antifa," *Washington Post*, September 11, 2020, https://www.washingtonpost.com/outlook/five-myths/five-myths-about-antifa/2020/09/11/527071ac-f37b-11ea-bc45-e5d48ab44b9f_story.html; Mark Bray, *Antifa: The Anti-Fascist Handbook* (Brooklyn: Melville House, 2017); Marisa Iati, "Two Senators Want Antifa Activists to Be Labeled 'Domestic Terrorists.' Here's What That Means," *Washington Post*, July 20, 2019, https://www.washingtonpost.com/politics/2019/07/20/senators-want-antifa-activists-be-labeled-domestic-terrorists-heres-what-that-means/; Adam Goldman, Katie Benner, and Zolan Kanno-Youngs, "How Trump's Focus on Antifa Distracted Attention from the Far-Right Threat," *New York Times*, January 30, 2021, https://www.nytimes.com/2021/01/30/us/politics/trump-right-wing-domestic-terrorism.html.
7 Donald Trump, "Remarks by President Trump before Marine One Departure," August 7, 2019, available at https://www.whitehouse.gov/briefings-statements/remarks-president-trump-marine-one-departure-58/.

8   Eileen Sullivan and Katie Benner, "White Supremacists Top Domestic Terror Threat, Officials Say," *New York Times*, May 12, 2021, https://www.nytimes.com/2021/05/12/us/politics/domestic-terror-white-supremacists.html; Robert O'Harrow Jr., Andrew Ba Tran, and Derek Hawkins, "The Rise of Domestic Extremism in America," *Washington Post*, April 12, 2021, https://www.washingtonpost.com/investigations/interactive/2021/domestic-terrorism-data/.
9   Aristotle, *Politics* 1313a34–1315b10; Livy, *History of Rome* 1.49, 56.1–3.
10 Adama Bah, "We Don't Need Another War on Terror," *New York Times*, January 25, 2021, https://www.nytimes.com/2021/01/25/opinion/domestic-terrorism-capitol-riots.html.

Chapter 12 Military misadventures abroad lead to instability at home

1   For this point and Pompey's career up to 60 BCE, see Dio, *Roman History* 36.30; Augustus, *Res Gestae* 1.1; Plutarch, *Pompey* 22–46; Seager, *Pompey* 40–62, 172.
2   Plutarch, *Crassus* 2.
3   Plutarch, *Pompey* 47–48, *Caesar* 14, *Cato* 33; Dio, *Roman History* 38.8.2.
4   Plutarch, *Caesar* 22, *Cato* 51; Caesar, *The Gallic Wars* 4.12–15; Kit Morrell, "Cato, Caesar, and the Germani," *Antichthon* 49 (2015): 73–93.
5   For Crassus' disastrous campaign against Parthia, see Plutarch, *Crassus* 16–33; Josephus, *Jewish Antiquities* 14.7.1; Allen Mason Ward, *Marcus Crassus and the Late Roman Republic* (Columbia: Columbia University Press, 1977), 231–88. For an analysis of these military ambitions and their analogies with America's War on Terror, see Nandini Pandey, "Rome's 'Empire without End' and the 'Endless' U.S. War on Terror," *Eidolon*, January 9, 2018, https://eidolon.pub/romes-empire-without-end-and-the-endless-u-s-war-on-terror-5c39ee3d0c66.
6   Lucan, *The Civil War* 1.125–126.
7   For the War on Terror and its early impact on America, see Jane Mayer, *The Dark Side: The Inside Story of How the War on Terror Turned into a War on American Ideals* (New York: Doubleday, 2008); Danny Goldberg, Victor Goldberg and Robert Greenwald, eds., *It's a Free Country: Personal Freedom in America after September 11* (New York: Thunder's Mouth Press/Nation Books, 2003); see also Pandey, "Rome's 'Empire Without End.'"
8   Brown University's Costs of War Project reports are available at https://watson.brown.edu/costsofwar/.
9   Thomas Gibbons-Neff, Eric Schmitt, and Helene Cooper, "Pentagon Accelerates Withdrawal from Afghanistan," *New York Times*, May 25, 2021, https://www.nytimes.com/2021/05/25/us/politics/us-afghanistan-withdrawal.html; Thomas Gibbons-Neff, "In Afghanistan, an Unceremonious End, and a Shrouded Beginning," *New York Times*, August 30, 2021, https://www.nytimes.com/2021/08/30/world/asia/us-withdrawal-afghanistan-kabul.html; Missy Ryan and Karen DeYoung, "Biden to Withdraw U.S. Forces from Afghanistan by Sept. 11, 2021," *Washington Post*, April 13, 2021, https://www.washingtonpost.com/national-security/biden-us-troop-witnhdrawal-afghanistan/2021/04/13/918c3cae-9beb-11eb-8a83-3bc1fa69c2e8_story.html; Alex Lubin, *Never-ending War on Terror* (Oakland, CA: University of California Press, 2021).

10 Reuters Staff, "Trump Pardon of Blackwater Iraq Contractors Violates International Law—UN," *Reuters*, December 30, 2020, https://www.reuters.com/article/us-iraq-blackwater-un/trump-pardon-of-blackwater-iraq-contractors-violates-international-law-un-idUSKBN294108; Falih Hassan and Jane Arraf, "Blackwater's Bullets Scarred Iraqis. Trump's Pardon Renewed the Pain," *New York Times*, January 7, 2021, https://www.nytimes.com/2020/12/23/world/middleeast/blackwater-trump-pardon.html.
11 Lauren Tierney, Tim Meko, Hannah Dormido, Laris Karklis, and Joe Fox, "Ahead of the Inauguration, Much of D.C. Closed Off Like Never Before," *Washington Post*, January 18, 2021, https://www.washingtonpost.com/dc-md-va/2021/01/15/ahead-inauguration-much-dc-closed-off-like-never-before/?arc404=true.

Chapter 13 Organized, armed gangs tear apart a political system

1 For Clodius and his political program, see Plutarch, *Cicero* 30–35; Dio, *Roman History* 38.13–17; Appian, *Civil Wars* 2.15-16; Watts, *Mortal Republic* 208–14; W. Jeffrey Tatum, *The Patrician Tribune: Publius Clodius Pulcher* (Chapel Hill: University of North Carolina Press, 2010).
2 Cicero, *Letters to Atticus* 4.3.4–5; Plutarch, *Cicero* 33–35.
3 For these events and the trial that followed, see Cicero, *Pro Milone*; Asconius, *Commentary on Cicero's Pro Milone* 26–36; Dio, *Roman History* 40.48–55; Appian, *Civil Wars* 2.20–24.
4 For the disruption of elections and Pompey as sole consul, see Plutarch, *Pompey* 54–55; *Caesar* 28; Asconius, *Commentary on Cicero's Pro Milone* 31; Dio, *Roman History* 40.44–56; Appian, *Civil Wars* 2.22-25; Seager, *Pompey* 101–51; Mackay, *Breakdown of the Roman Republic* 274–77; Watts, *Mortal Republic* 212–14.
5 Dio, *Roman History* 42.22–25; Caesar, *Civil Wars* 3.20–22.
6 James H. Madison, *The Ku Klux Klan in the Heartland* (Bloomington: Indiana University Press, 2020); Michael Newton, *White Robes and Burning Crosses: A History of the Ku Klux Klan from 1866* (Jefferson, NC: McFarland, 2014).
7 S. Paul O'Hara, *Inventing the Pinkertons or, Spies, Sleuths, Mercenaries, and Thugs: Being a Story of the Nation's Most Famous (and Infamous) Detective Agency* (Baltimore: Johns Hopkins University Press, 2016).
8 Hal Bernton, "Jury Acquits Leaders of Malheur Wildlife-Refuge Standoff," *Seattle Times*, October 27, 2016, https://www.seattletimes.com/seattle-news/crime/verdict-near-in-malheur-wildlife-refuge-standoff-trial/; Leah Sottile, "Malheur Wildlife Refuge Occupation Still Reverberating as FBI Agent Goes on Trial," *Washington Post*, July 25, 2018, https://www.washingtonpost.com/national/malheur-wildlife-refuge-occupation-still-reverberating-as-fbi-agent-goes-on-trial/2018/07/25/3b6c2f18-8f5b-11e8-8322-b5482bf5e0f5_story.html.
9 Rosie Gray, "Trump Defends White-Nationalist Protesters: 'Some Very Fine People on Both Sides,'" *Atlantic*, August 15, 2017, https://www.theatlantic.com/politics/archive/2017/08/trump-defends-white-nationalist-protesters-some-very-fine-people-on-both-sides/537012/.
10 For these heavily armed protests throughout the United States in 2020, see Washington Post Staff, "Thousands of Gun Rights Advocates Rally in Virginia Capital," *Washington Post*, January 20, 2020, https://www.washingtonpost.com/graphics/2020/local/amp-stories/virginia-gun-rally/; Jonathan Bullington, Sarah Ladd, and

Billy Kobin, "Crowd at Kentucky Capitol Gun Rally Says the Second Amendment Is under Attack," *Louisville Courier Journal*, January 31, 2020, https://www.courier-journal.com/story/news/politics/2020/01/31/kentucky-gun-rights-rally-calls-protecting-second-amendment/2858260001/.

11 Nicholas Bogel-Burroughs, Shaila Dewan, and Kathleen Gray, "F.B.I. Says Michigan Anti-Government Group Plotted to Kidnap Gov. Gretchen Whitmer," *New York Times*, November 3, 2020, https://www.nytimes.com/2020/10/08/us/gretchen-whitmer-michigan-militia.html; John Flesher, "6 Men Indicted in Alleged Plot to Kidnap Michigan Governor," *Associated Press*, December 17, 2020, https://apnews.com/article/gretchen-whitmer-michigan-indictments-coronavirus-pandemic-traverse-city-10f7e02c57004da9843f89650edd4510; Maegan Vazquez and Nikki Carvajal, "Trump Appears to Give a Pass to the Domestic Kidnapping Plot against Whitmer," *CNN*, October 27, 2020, https://www.cnn.com/2020/10/27/politics/trump-gretchen-whitmer-kidnapping-michigan/index.html; Gretchen Whitmer, "The Plot to Kidnap Me," *Atlantic*, October 27, 2020, https://www.theatlantic.com/ideas/archive/2020/10/plot-kidnap-me/616866/; Maggie Haberman, Jim Rutenberg, Nick Corasaniti, and Reid J. Epstein, "Trump Targets Michigan in His Ploy to Subvert the Election," *New York Times*, November 19, 2020, https://www.nytimes.com/2020/11/19/us/politics/trump-michigan-election.html.

12 For events in Oregon, Charlottesville, the Proud Boys, and the Capitol, see Maxine Bernstein, "Armed Occupation of Malheur Refuge Was 'Dress Rehearsal' for Violent Takeover of Nation's Capitol, Extremist Watchdogs Say," *Oregonian*, January 8, 2021, https://www.oregonlive.com/crime/2021/01/armed-occupation-of-malheur-refuge-was-dress-rehearsal-for-violent-takeover-of-nations-capitol-extremist-watchdogs-say.html; Louis P. Nelson and Claudrena N. Harold, *Charlottesville 2017: The Legacy of Race and Inequity* (Charlottesville: University of Virginia Press, 2018); Ben Collins and Brandy Zadrozny, "Proud Boys Celebrate after Trump's Debate Callout," *NBC News*, September 30, 2020, https://www.nbcnews.com/tech/tech-news/proud-boys-celebrate-after-trump-s-debate-call-out-n1241512; Rebecca Boone, "Armed Statehouse Protests Set Tone for US Capitol Insurgents," *Associated Press*, January 7, 2021, https://apnews.com/article/election-2020-coronavirus-pandemic-oregon-elections-idaho-688fc8894f44992487bb6ee45e9abd77.

Chapter 14 Institutions may not be able to save the republic

1 For Caesar's candidacy for the consulship in absentia, see Cicero *Letters to Atticus* 7.1.4, 8.3.3; Appian, *Civil Wars* 2.25; Dio, *Roman History* 40.51; Seager, *Pompey* 138-39; Mackay, *Breakdown of the Roman Republic* 279–83.

2 For the debate over Caesar's return and the surrounding negotiations, see Caesar, *Gallic Wars* 8.50-55, *Civil Wars* 1.1–5; Plutarch, *Pompey* 58–61, *Caesar* 29–32; Appian, *Civil Wars* 2.30–31; Dio, *Roman History* 40.58–41.3; Mackay, *Breakdown of the Roman Republic* 277–88; Watts, *Mortal Republic* 215–17.

3 Andrew Restuccia, Burgess Everett, and Heather Caygle, "Longest Shutdown in History Ends after Trump Relents on Wall," *Politico*, January 25, 2018, https://www.politico.com/story/2019/01/25/trump-shutdown-announcement-1125529; for the recent government shutdowns generally, see Editorial Board, "Congress Shouldn't Need a Crisis to Do Its Job," *New York Times*, July 23, 2019, https://www.nytimes.com/2019/07/23/opinion/end-debt-ceiling.html.

4   Nicholas Fandos, "Senate Republicans Filibuster Jan. 6 Inquiry Bill, Blocking an Investigation," *New York Times*, May 28, 2021, https://www.nytimes.com/2021/05/28/us/politics/capitol-riot-commission-republicans.html; Adam Jentleson, *Kill Switch: The Rise of the Modern Senate and the Crippling of American Democracy* (New York: Liveright, 2021).
5   John Cannan, "A Legislative History of the Affordable Care Act: How Legislative Procedure Shapes Legislative History," *Law Library Journal* 105 no. 2 (2013): 131-173; Center on Budget and Policy Priorities, "Sabotage Watch: Tracking Efforts to Undermine the ACA," available at https://www.cbpp.org/sabotage-watch-tracking-efforts-to-undermine-the-aca.
6   Sahil Kapur and Frank Thorp V, "What Is Budget Reconciliation: An Explainer on the Fast-track Process for Covid Relief," *NBC News*, February 6, 2021, https://www.nbcnews.com/politics/congress/what-budget-reconciliation-explainer-fast-track-process-covid-relief-n1256592.
7   There is brief mention of a plague early in the reign of Augustus in 23–22 BCE, but there is only one source who provides only one line on this plague, so it does not seem to have had a profound impact on Rome, and seems to have been used largely as a ploy for bolstering Augustus's power. Dio, *Roman History* 54.1; Pat Southern, *Augustus*, 2nd edition (New York: Routledge, 2014), 125–26; Watts, *Mortal Republic* 276–78.
8   For an ancient analogue to the threat that COVID-19 has posed to American democracy, we should turn to ancient Athens, which suffered a plague of great magnitude for several successive years beginning in 430 BCE. At the height of its power and in the midst of the Peloponnesian War, democratic Athens was brought to its knees and never fully recovered its political health for a generation. For the account of the plague of Athens, see Thucydides, *Peloponnesian War* 2.47–54. See also, Thomas Strunk, "Reading Thucydides in a Time of Pandemic," *Liberation Now*, March 22, 2020, https://www.LiberationNow.org/reading-thucydides-in-a-time-of-pandemic/.
9   William Rosen, *Justinian's Flea: The First Great Plague and the End of the Roman Empire* (New York: Penguin Random House, 2008). For the plague under Marcus Aurelius, see Kyle Harper, "Ancient Rome Has an Urgent Warning for Us," *New York Times*, February 16, 2021, https://www.nytimes.com/2021/02/15/opinion/ancient-rome-covid.html.
10 For the failures of the US health system, see Timothy Snyder, *Our Malady: Lessons in Liberty from a Hospital Diary* (New York: Crown, 2020).
11 Much has been written about the coronavirus and much more will need to be written; for the points mentioned here, see Oliver Milman, "Trump Administration Cut Pandemic Early Warning Program in September," *Guardian*, April 3, 2020, https://www.theguardian.com/world/2020/apr/03/trump-scrapped-pandemic-early-warning-program-system-before-coronavirus; David Quammen, "Why Weren't We Ready for the Coronavirus?," *New Yorker*, May 4, 2020, https://www.newyorker.com/magazine/2020/05/11/why-werent-we-ready-for-the-coronavirus; Ed Yong, "How the Pandemic Defeated America," *Atlantic*, August 4, 2020, https://www.theatlantic.com/magazine/archive/2020/09/coronavirus-american-failure/614191/; Yasmeen Abutaleb, Ashley Parker, Josh Dawsey, and Philip Rucker, "The Inside Story of How Trump's Denial, Mismanagement and Magical Thinking Led to the Pandemic's Dark Winter," *Washington Post*, December 19, 2020, https://www.washingtonpost.com/graphics/2020/politics/trump-covid-pandemic-dark-winter/.
12 Donald Moynihan and Gregory Porumbescu, "Trump's 'Chinese Virus' Slur Makes Some People Blame Chinese Americans. But Others Blame Trump," *Washington Post*, September 16, 2020, https://www.washingtonpost.com/politics/2020/09/16/trumps-chinese-virus-slur-makes-some-people-blame-chinese-americans-others-blame-trump/;

Darlene Superville, "Biden Signs Bill to Counter Spike in Anti-Asian Hate Crime," *Washington Post*, May 20, 2021, https://www.washingtonpost.com/politics/biden-signs-bill-to-counter-spike-in-anti-asian-hate-crime/2021/05/20/d419da40-b9aa-11eb-bc4a-62849cf6cca9_story.html; Sam Cabral, "Covid 'Hate Crimes' against Asian Americans on Rise," *BBC News*, May 21, 2021, https://www.bbc.com/news/world-us-canada-56218684.

13 For the political and social impact of pandemics, see Marc Fisher, "Eroding Trust, Spreading Fear: The Historical Ties between Pandemics and Extremism," *Washington Post*, February 15, 2021, https://www.washingtonpost.com/politics/pandemics-spawn-extremism/2021/02/14/d4f7195c-6b1f-11eb-ba56-d7e2c8defa31_story.html; Lois Beckett, "Armed Protesters Demonstrate against Covid-19 Lockdown at Michigan Capitol," *Guardian*, April, 30, 2020, https://www.theguardian.com/us-news/2020/apr/30/michigan-protests-coronavirus-lockdown-armed-capitol; Jane Kaufman, "Protesters Picket Dr. Amy Acton's Home for Third Time," *Cleveland Jewish News*, May 9, 2020, https://www.clevelandjewishnews.com/news/local_news/protesters-picket-dr-amy-actons-home-for-third-time/article_d2025d20-925c-11ea-9e10-732d28564173.html.

14 Ed Yong, "What Happens When Americans Can Finally Exhale," *Atlantic*, May 20, 2021, https://www.theatlantic.com/health/archive/2021/05/pandemic-trauma-summer/618934/; Ed Yong, "Where the Pandemic Will Take America in 2021," *Atlantic*, December 29, 2020, https://www.theatlantic.com/health/archive/2020/12/pandemic-year-two/617528/.

15 For vaccine hesitancy, see Blake Farmer, "'It's Not a Never Thing'—White, Rural Southerners Remain Hesitant to Get COVID Vaccine," *NPR*, April 15, 2021, https://www.npr.org/sections/health-shots/2021/04/15/987412681/its-not-a-never-thing-white-rural-southerners-are-waiting-to-get-the-vaccine; Dan Royles, "Years of Medical Abuse Make Black Americans Less Likely to Trust the Coronavirus Vaccine," *Washington Post*, December 15, 2020, https://www.washingtonpost.com/outlook/2020/12/15/years-medical-abuse-make-black-americans-less-likely-trust-covid-vaccine/; Brenda Leon, "To Address Vaccine Hesitancy Among Latinos, A Trusted Source Is Key," *Connecticut Public Radio*, February 1, 2021, https://www.wnpr.org/post/address-vaccine-hesitancy-among-latinos-trusted-source-key.

16 Recently published, but too late to be consulted here, are Michael Lewis, *The Premonition: A Pandemic Story* (New York: W.W. Norton, 2021); Lawrence Wright, *The Plague Year* (New York: Alfred A. Knopf, 2021).

Chapter 15 A tyrant backed into a corner is a danger to the republic

1 For the Roman triumph, see Mary Beard, *The Roman Triumph* (Cambridge, MA: Harvard University Press, 2007).
2 Dio, *Roman History* 40.60.
3 Lucan, *The Civil War* 1.8-23.
4 For the Department of Justice, Office of Legal Counsel's opinion against indicting a sitting president, see https://www.justice.gov/olc/opinion/sitting-president%E2%80%99s-amenability-indictment-and-criminal-prosecution.

5 Carol D. Leonnig and Tom Hamburger, "Mueller's Approach to Question of Whether Trump Obstructed Justice Leaves Both Sides Frustrated," *Washington Post*, July 24, 2019, https://www.washingtonpost.com/politics/muellers-approach-to-question-of-whether-trump-obstructed-justice-leaves-both-sides-frustrated/2019/07/24/74621fb6-ad79-11e9-bc5c-e73b603e7f38_story.html; Lawrence Douglas, "Robert Mueller Made Clear: He Couldn't Have Indicted Trump Even If He Wanted To," *Guardian*, May 30, 2019, https://www.theguardian.com/commentisfree/2019/may/30/robert-mueller-trump-statement.

6 Katie Shepherd, "Democrats on FEC Blast Decision to Drop Probe into Trump Hush-Money Payment to Stormy Daniels: 'Defies Reality,'" *Washington Post*, May 6, 2021, https://www.washingtonpost.com/nation/2021/05/06/fec-trump-stormy-daniels-cohen/.

7 Spencer S. Hsu, "Justice Dept. Asks Judge to Toss Lawsuit against Trump, Barr for Violent Clearing of Lafayette Square," *Washington Post*, May 28, 2021, https://www.washingtonpost.com/local/legal-issues/trump-lafayette-square-civil-lawsuit/2021/05/28/c413c840-bfb3-11eb-b26e-53663e6be6ff_story.html.

8 Danny Hakim, William K. Rashbaum, and Ben Protess, "New York's Attorney General Joins Criminal Inquiry into Trump Organization," *New York Times*, May 18, 2021, https://www.nytimes.com/2021/05/18/nyregion/trump-ny-ag-investigation-vance.html?action=click&module=Top%20Stories&pgtype=Homepage; Richard Fausset and Danny Hakim, "Georgia Prosecutors Open Criminal Inquiry into Trump's Efforts to Subvert Election," *New York Times*, February 10, 2021, https://www.nytimes.com/2021/02/10/us/politics/trump-georgia-investigation.html?action=click&module=RelatedLinks&pgtype=Article.

9 Shayna Jacobs, Devlin Barrett, and Josh Dawsey, "Federal Agents Execute Search Warrant at Giuliani's Home," *Washington Post*, April 28, 2021, https://www.washingtonpost.com/national-security/rudy-giuliani-search-warrant/2021/04/28/e5ba6ed2-a83d-11eb-bca5-048b2759a489_story.html.

Chapter 16 The real problem is not simply a tyrannical leader

1 Dio, *Roman History* 43.45.3; Suetonius, *Caesar* 76–79.
2 For the complexities of the tradition, see Herodotus, *Histories* 5.55, 62–65; Thucydides, *Peloponnesian War* 5.54–59.
3 Shakespeare used Thomas North's translation of Plutarch's *Lives* as his historical source for *Julius Caesar*. William Shakespeare, *Julius Caesar*, ed. David Daniell (London: Bloomsbury, 2014), 79–94; Stephen Greenblatt, *Tyrant: Shakespeare on Politics* (New York: W.W. Norton, 2018), 147–54.
4 For the events surrounding the Lupercalia and Caesar's assassination, see Plutarch, *Caesar* 61–69, *Brutus* 10-20; Suetonius, *Caesar* 79–89; Dio, *Roman History* 44.1–22; Appian, *Civil Wars* 2.107–118; for accounts that examine these events and the broader implications, see Barry Strauss, *The Death of Caesar: The Story of History's Most Famous Assassination* (New York: Simon & Schuster, 2015); Greg Woolf, *Et Tu Brute? A Short History of Political Murder* (Cambridge, MA: Harvard University Press, 2007).
5 Shakespeare, *Julius Caesar* 1.2.158–160.

6. Barbara McQuade, "What Would Happen If Trump Refused to Leave Office?," *Atlantic*, February 22, 2020, https://www.theatlantic.com/ideas/archive/2020/02/what-if-he-wont-go/606259/.
7. John Eligon and Thomas Kaplan, "These Are the Republicans Who Voted to Impeach Trump," *New York Times*, January 23, 2021, https://www.nytimes.com/article/republicans-impeaching-donald-trump.html; Luke Broadwater, "Here Are the Seven Republicans Who Voted to Convict Trump," *New York Times*, February 13, 2021, https://www.nytimes.com/2021/02/13/us/politics/republicans-vote-to-impeach.html.
8. Martin Pengelly, "Trump Quotes Emerson: 'When You Strike at the King, You Must Kill Him,'" *Guardian*, February 15, 2020, https://www.theguardian.com/us-news/2020/feb/15/donald-trump-new-york-times-grievance-persecution-resentment-daytona-500.
9. Jonathan Easley, "Trump on Acquittal 'MAGA Has Only Just Begun,'" *Hill*, February 13, 2021, https://thehill.com/homenews/senate/538766-trump-on-acquittal-maga-has-just-begun?rl=1.
10. The origins of the present crisis in the United States is open to debate; Levistsky and Ziblatt, *How Democracies Die*, 146–49, trace the origins of the present crisis back to the rise of Newt Gingrich in large part. Another potential point of origin is the presidency of Ronald Reagan, who fomented distrust in government and drove economic policies that greatly debilitated unions and the middle-class. For a perspective that views Reagan's America as "the summertime of American resurgence," see Nick Bryant, *When America Stopped Being Great: A History of the Present* (London: Bloomsbury Continuum, 2021), 17.

Chapter 17 Free speech can disappear

1. For Cicero and the events following Caesar's assassination, see Plutarch, *Cicero* 42–49, *Antony* 15-20; Suetonius, *Augustus* 10–12; Rawson 1975, 260–98; Watts, *Mortal Republic* 240–59.
2. Levitsky and Ziblatt, *How Democracies Die*, 11–32, identify Mussolini, Hitler, and Hugo Chavez as examples of outsiders whom elder politicians thought they could control.
3. For the suspicions around the death of Hirtius and Pansa, see Cicero, *Letters to Brutus* 1.6.2; Tacitus, *Annals* 1.10.2; Suetonius, *Augustus* 11.
4. Appian, *Civil Wars* 3.86–88; Dio, *Roman History* 46.36–40.
5. Plutarch, *Antony* 19–20; Appian, *Civil Wars* 4.1–7; Dio, *Roman History* 47.1–14.
6. For Cicero's murder, see Plutarch, *Cicero* 47–48; *Antony* 20; Seneca the Elder, *Suasoriae* 6; Appian, *Civil Wars* 4.19–20; Dio, *Roman History* 47.8.
7. Tacitus, *Annals* 1.1. For the loss of free speech under the Roman Empire, see Strunk, *History after Liberty*, 133–65.
8. Trump used this language throughout his campaign and presidency. For one example a week before the 2020 election, see Diane Rado, "Trump Calls America's Free Press 'the Enemy of the People,'" *Florida Phoenix*, October 29, 2020, https://www.floridaphoenix.com/blog/trump-calls-americas-free-press-the-enemy-of-the-people/. For the anti-semitic and fascist roots of Trump's attack on the press, see Rick Noack, "The Ugly History of 'Lügenpresse,' a Nazi Slur Shouted at a Trump Rally," *Washington Post*, October 24, 2016, https://www.washingtonpost.com/news/worldviews/wp/2016/10/24/the-ugly-history-of-luegenpresse-a-nazi-slur-shouted-at-a-trump-rally/.

9   Timothy Williams, "Suspect in Capital Gazette Shooting Pleads Guilty," *New York Times*, October 28, 2019, https://www.nytimes.com/2019/10/28/us/jarrod-ramos-guilty-capital-gazette.html.
10 Julia Carrie Wong and Sam Levin, "Republican Candidate Charged with Assault after 'Body-Slamming' Guardian Reporter," *Guardian*, May 25, 2017, https://www.theguardian.com/us-news/2017/may/24/greg-gianforte-bodyslams-reporter-ben-jacobs-montana.
11 Elahe Izadi, "Rare Trial of U.S. Journalist Arrested on the Job Begins in Iowa," *Washington Post*, March 8, 2021, https://www.washingtonpost.com/media/2021/03/08/iowa-reporter-trial/; Devlin Barrett, "Trump Justice Department Secretly Obtained Post Reporters' Phone Records," *Washington Post*, May 7, 2021, https://www.washingtonpost.com/national-security/trump-justice-dept-seized-post-reporters-phone-records/2021/05/07/933cdfc6-af5b-11eb-b476-c3b287e52a01_story.html; Adam Goldman, "Trump Justice Dept. Seized CNN Reporter's Email and Phone Records," *New York Times*, May 20, 2021, https://www.nytimes.com/2021/05/20/us/politics/cnn-trump-barbara-starr.html; Margaret Sullivan, "Trump Is Leaving Press Freedom in Tatters. Biden Can Take These Bold Steps to Repair the Damage," *Washington Post*, December 6, 2020, https://www.washingtonpost.com/lifestyle/media/trump-biden-press-freedom/2020/12/04/251c669e-3583-11eb-a997-1f4c53d2a747_story.html; Editorial Board, "Journalism Got More Dangerous in 2020—including in the United States," *Washington Post*, December 27, 2020, https://www.washingtonpost.com/opinions/global-opinions/journalism-got-more-dangerous-in-2020--including-in-the-united-states/2020/12/25/8b439dac-4154-11eb-8db8-395dedaaa036_story.html.
12 Brittany Shammas, "Journalists Were Attacked, Threatened and Detained during the Capitol Siege," *Washington Post*, January 9, 2021, https://www.washingtonpost.com/media/2021/01/09/he-was-documenting-chaotic-scene-when-suddenly-trump-supporters-turned-their-ire-him/. For the number of assaults on journalists and violations against freedom of the press, see US Press Freedom Tracker at https://pressfreedomtracker.us/.

Chapter 18 The crisis can be manufactured to continue

1 Suetonius, *Julius Caesar* 88; Plutarch, *Caesar* 69; Dio, *Roman History* 45.7; J.T. Ramsey and A.L. Licht, *The Comet of 44 BC and Caesar's Funeral Games* (Oxford: Oxford University Press, 1997); Michael Koortbojian, *The Divinization of Caesar and Augustus: Precedents, Consequences, Implications* (Cambridge: Cambridge University Press, 2013).
2 For the events following Caesar's assassination and Philippi, see Tacitus, *Annals* 1.2; Suetonius, *Augustus* 1–12; Plutarch, *Antony* 14–22, *Brutus* 18–53; Appian, *Civil Wars* Books 3–4; Dio, *Roman History* 44.23–47; Kathryn Tempest, *Brutus: The Noble Conspirator* (New Haven: Yale University Press, 2017), 105–210. For these details on Augustus, and generally, see Southern, *Augustus* 21–65.
3 For the Second Triumvirate, see Plutarch, *Antony* 23–52; Suetonius, *Augustus* 13–16; Dio, *Roman History* 48–49.33; Appian, *Civil Wars* Book 5; Watts, *Mortal Republic* 258–70.
4 For Antony's will, the Donations of Alexandria and Cleopatra, see Suetonius, *Augustus* 17; Plutarch, *Antony* 54, 58; Dio *Roman History* 50.3–5, 20.

5   Augustus, *Res Gestae* 25.2; Suetonius, *Augustus* 17.2; Dio, *Roman History* 50.6.6; Syme, *Roman Revolution* 284; Southern, *Augustus* 96–97.
6   Augustus, *Res Gestae* 34; Velleius Paterculus, *Roman History* 2.91; Tacitus, *Annals* 1.1–5; Plutarch, *Ant.* 53–87; Suetonius, *Augustus* 7, 17; Dio, *Roman History* Book 51; Southern, *Augustus* 100–17.
7   Jeanne Sahadi, "The Covid Divide: The Pandemic Has Plunged Some into Poverty, and Boosted Savings for Others," *CNN*, December 10, 2020, https://www.cnn.com/2020/12/10/success/covid-divide-personal-economy/index.html.
8   Brent Kendall, "Trump Says Judge's Mexican Heritage Presents 'Absolute Conflict,'" *Wall Street Journal*, June 3, 2016, https://www.wsj.com/articles/donald-trump-keeps-up-attacks-on-judge-gonzalo-curiel-1464911442; Jia Tolentino, "Trump and the Truth: The 'Mexican' Judge,'" *New Yorker*, September 20, 2016, https://www.newyorker.com/news/news-desk/trump-and-the-truth-the-mexican-judge.
9   Mishal Reja, "Trump's 'Chinese Virus' Tweet Helped Lead to Rise in Racist Anti-Asian Twitter Content: Study," *ABC News*, March 18, 2021, https://abcnews.go.com/Health/trumps-chinese-virus-tweet-helped-lead-rise-racist/story?id=76530148; Justine Coleman, "Photo of Trump's Notes Shows 'Chinese' Virus Written over 'Coronavirus,'" *Hill*, March 19, 2020, https://thehill.com/homenews/administration/488502-photo-of-trumps-notes-shows-chinese-virus-written-over-coronavirus.
10 For Trump's hyper-masculinity, see Danielle Kurtzleben, "Trump Has Weaponized Masculinity as President. Here's Why It Matters," *NPR: Weekend Edition Saturday*, October 28, 2020, https://www.npr.org/2020/10/28/928336749/trump-has-weaponized-masculinity-as-president-heres-why-it-matters; Danielle Kurtzleben, "Masculinity's Big Role in Trump's Presidency," *NPR: Weekend Edition Sunday*, January 17, 2021, https://www.npr.org/2021/01/17/957779157/masculinitys-big-role-in-trumps-presidency.
11 Jeanine Santucci, "Trump to Women at Michigan Rally: 'We're Getting Your Husbands Back to Work,'" *USA Today*, October 28, 2020, https://www.usatoday.com/story/news/politics/2020/10/27/president-trump-rally-women-were-getting-your-husbands-back-work/3755175001/; Katie Rogers, "2.5 Million Women Left the Work Force During the Pandemic. Harris Sees a 'National Emergency,'" *New York Times*, February 18, 2021, https://www.nytimes.com/2021/02/18/us/politics/women-pandemic-harris.html.
12 Monica Hesse, "What Do 'Lock Her Up' and 'Send Her Back' Have in Common? It's Pretty Obvious," *Washington Post*, July 20, 2019, https://www.washingtonpost.com/lifestyle/style/what-do-lock-her-up-and-send-her-back-have-in-common-its-pretty-obvious/2019/07/19/74bc4790-a999-11e9-9214-246e594de5d5_story.html.
13 For catalogues of these transgressions, see Amy Siskind, *The Weekly List: This Is How Democracy Ends*, available at https://theweeklylist.org/; see also Amy Siskind, "This Is Not Normal," *Washington Post*, October 16, 2020; Ben Parker, et al., *Lest We Forget the Horrors: A Catalog of Trump's Worst Cruelties, Collusions, Corruptions, and Crimes*, available at https://www.mcsweeneys.net/columns/reasons-why-donald-trump-is-unfit-to-be-president.
14 Adrienne LaFrance, "The Prophecies of Q," *Atlantic*, June 2020, https://www.theatlantic.com/magazine/archive/2020/06/qanon-nothing-can-stop-what-is-coming/610567/; Ben Sasse, "QAnon Is Destroying the GOP from Within," *Atlantic*, January 16, 2021, https://www.theatlantic.com/ideas/archive/2021/01/conspiracy-theories-will-doom-republican-party/617707/.

Chapter 19 The revolution can be advertised as a restoration

1. Augustus, *Res Gestae* 1–2, 34; Augustus's assertion is echoed by Velleius Paterculus, *Roman History* 2.89.3.
2. Appian, *Civil Wars* 5.132; Suetonius, *Augustus* 28.
3. Augustus, *Res Gestae* 19–21; Suetonius, *Augustus* 28.
4. Tacitus, *Annals* 1.1.1.
5. Tacitus, *Annals* 1.1–15; Dio, *Roman History* Book 52.
6. For the points here and Augustus's rule generally, Suetonius, *Augustus*; Dio, *Roman History* Books 53–56; Watts, *Mortal Republic* 271–80; Mackay, *Breakdown of the Roman Republic* 362–402; Southern, *Augustus* 100–80.
7. For Trump's thousands of lies, see Glenn Kessler, "Trump Made 30,573 False or Misleading Claims as President. Nearly Half Came in His Final Year," *Washington Post*, January 23, 2021, https://www.washingtonpost.com/politics/2021/01/24/trumps-false-or-misleading-claims-total-30573-over-four-years/.

Chapter 20 Freedom lost cannot so easily be regained

1. Tacitus, *Agricola* 3.1.
2. Tacitus, *Annals* 4.34–35.
3. For obeying in advance, see Timothy Snyder, *On Tyranny: Twenty Lessons from the Twentieth Century* (New York: Tim Duggan Books, 2017), 17–21. For Roman self-censorship and adulation, see Strunk, *History after Liberty*, 133–46; Daniel J. Kapust, *Flattery and the History of Political Thought: That Glib and Oily Art* (Cambridge: Cambridge University Press, 2018), 30–63.
4. For the elimination of Roman elections, see Tacitus, *Annals* 1.14–15, 1.81. The last consul in the Western Roman Empire was Decius Paulinus in 534 CE and Anicius Faustus Albinus Basilius in 541 CE in the Eastern Roman Empire (Byzantine Empire).
5. Tacitus, *Annals* 3.65.3, *O homines ad servitutem paratos!* For the sycophancy of the imperial senate, see Strunk, *History after Liberty*, 133–46. For the imperial senate generally, see Richard J. A. Talbert, *The Senate of Imperial Rome* (Princeton: Princeton University Press, 1984).
6. Suetonius, *Caligula* 55, *Nero* 23; Tacitus, *Annals* 14.1–13, *Agricola* 1–3, 45–46.

Conclusion

1. Annie Karni and Jonathan Martin, "Lara Trump for North Carolina Senate Seat? Trump's Trial Is Renewing Talk," *New York Times*, February 14, 2021, https://www.nytimes.com/2021/02/14/us/politics/lara-trump-north-carolina.html.
2. Zeynep Tufekci, "America's Next Authoritarian Will Be Much More Competent," *Atlantic*, November 6, 2020, https://www.theatlantic.com/ideas/archive/2020/11/trump-proved-authoritarians-can-get-elected-america/617023/.
3. David Brooks, "What the Voters Are Trying to Tell Us," *New York Times*, November 5, 2020, https://www.nytimes.com/2020/11/05/opinion/trump-biden-voters.html.

BIBLIOGRAPHIC NOTE

Ancient sources

For most ancient authors I have cited accessible, reliable, and readily available translations. Those interested in the original Latin or Greek should consult the Loeb Classical Library for the author in question.

Appian. *The Civil Wars*. Trans. Horace White. Cambridge, MA: Harvard University Press, 1961.
Augustus. *Res Gestae Divi Augusti: Text, Translation, and Commentary*. Ed. Alison E. Cooley. Cambridge: Cambridge University Press, 2009.
Caesar. *The Landmark Julius Caesar: The Complete Works*. Trans. Kurt A. Raaflaub. New York: Pantheon Books, 2017.
Cassius Dio. *The Roman History: The Reign of Augustus*. Trans. Ian Scott-Kilvert. London: Penguin Books, 1987. Cassius Dio is simply referred to as Dio throughout the notes.
Cicero. *In Defence of the Republic*. Trans. Siobhán McElduff. London: Penguin Books, 2011.
Herodotus. *The Histories*. Trans. Pamela Mensch. Indianapolis: Hackett, 2014.
Livy. *The History of Rome: Books 1–5*. Trans. Valerie M. Warrior. Indianapolis: Hackett, 2006.
Livy. *Rome's Mediterranean Empire: Books 41–45 and The Periochae*. Trans. Jane D. Chaplin. Oxford: Oxford University Press, 2007.
Plutarch. *The Fall of the Roman Republic*. Trans. Rex Warner. London: Penguin Books, 2005.
Plutarch. *Rome in Crisis*. Trans. Ian Scott-Kilvert and Christopher Pelling. London: Penguin Books, 2010.
Polybius. *The Histories*. Trans. Robin Waterfield. Oxford: Oxford University Press, 2010.
Sallust. *Catiline's War, The Jugurthine War, Histories*. Trans. A. J. Woodman. London: Penguin Books, 2007.
Suetonius. *The Twelve Caesars*. Trans. Robert Graves. London: Penguin Books, 2003.
Tacitus. *Agricola, Germany, and Dialogue on Orators*. Trans. Herbert W. Benario. Indianapolis: Hackett, 2006.
Tacitus. *The Annals*. Trans. A. J. Woodman. Indianapolis: Hackett, 2004.
Tacitus. *The Histories*. Trans. W. H. Fyfe. Oxford: Oxford University Press, 2008.
Thucydides. *The Peloponnesian War*. Trans. Steven Lattimore. Indianapolis: Hackett, 1998.
Velleius Paterculus. *The Roman History*. Trans. J. C. Yardley and Anthony A. Barrett. Indianapolis: Hackett, 2011.

Modern Sources on Ancient Events

Mackay, Christopher S. *The Breakdown of the Roman Republic: From Oligarchy to Empire.* Cambridge: Cambridge University Press, 2009.

Scullard, H.H. *From the Gracchi to Nero: A History of Rome 133 BC to AD 68.* London: Routledge, 2011.

Syme, Ronald. *The Roman Revolution.* Oxford: Oxford University Press, 1939.

Taylor, Lily Ross. *Party Politics in the Age of Caesar.* Berkeley: University of California Press, 1966.

Watts, Edward J. *Mortal Republic: How Rome Fell into Tyranny.* New York: Basic Books, 2018.

Modern Sources on Modern Events

For sources on the modern events, please see the citations in the notes. Any particular topic is easily searchable. I would recommend news media such as the *New York Times*, the *Washington Post, Politico,* the *Atlantic,* and the *Guardian* as places to start. However, most of the modern events discussed here are not items of great controversy, and news coverage, along with video in many cases, can be readily found at BBC, Fox News, MSNBC, ABC, CBS, NBC, CNN, NPR, C-SPAN, and others.

INDEX

Actium 83
Acton, Amy 68
Adams, Abigail 95
Aeneas 33
Affordable Care Act 67
Afghanistan 59–60, 83
al-Awlaki, Abdulrahman 54
al-Awlaki, Anwar 54
al-Awlaki, Nawar 54
anacyclosis 6, 8, 93, 98
antifa 55
antisemitism 1
Antonius, Gaius 49, 50
Antony, Mark 10, 74, 77–78, 81–83, 85
Appian Way 46, 62
aristocracy 6
Aristogeiton 73
Aristotle 6, 55
Asian Americans and Pacific Islanders 25, 68, 84
assemblies, Roman 6–7, 9, 22–23, 29, 39, 49, 54, 61, 81
Athenion 45
Athens xvi, 117n8
   tyrannicide 73
Atlanta spa shooting 25, 63
Attalus III 21
Augustus 5, 10, 14, 27, 30, 57, 77–78, 81–83, 85–87, 89, 90, 93
   elites 90
   first consulship 27, 57, 86
   imperator 86
   loyalty oath 82–83
   princeps 85, 86
   Res Gestae 10, 85, 86
authoritarianism 1, 2, 11, 15, 53

autocracy 2, 10, 13, 14, 20, 21, 27, 83, 89, 90, 93, 94

Baghdad 60
Barrett, Amy Coney 11
Battle of Blair Mountain 25
Best, Ricky 25
Biden, Joe 11, 31, 37, 41, 47, 51, 52, 84, 93
bin Laden, Osama 60
Black Americans 35, 47–48, 76
Black Lives Matter 31, 55, 76
Blackwater 60
Brooks, David 94
Brutus, Lucius—the Liberator 2, 85
Brutus, Marcus—the tyrannicide 10, 14, 73–75, 77–78, 81–82, 89
Bush, George W. 36, 59

Caesar, Julius 5, 10, 28, 30, 53–54, 57–59, 73–75, 81–82, 93, 94
   assassination 10, 14, 73–74
   civil war 5, 65–66, 69–70, 73, 74, 77
   dictatorship 41, 73, 74, 85–86, 93
   Gallic campaigns 58–59
Caligula, Gaius 90
Camillus xvi, 97n4
Capital Gazette shooting 79
Capitol insurrection 11, 19, 25, 30, 41–44, 47, 52, 55, 60, 64, 79
Capitoline Hill 21, 73
Caracalla 33
CARES Act 67
Carrhae 59, 62
Carthage 17
Cassidy, Bill 55

Cassius Longinus, Gaius 10, 14, 59, 73–75, 77–78, 81–82, 89
Catilinarian Conspiracy 50, 53, 77
Catiline, Lucius Sergius 49–50
Cato, Marcus Porcius 50, 53–54, 58, 66, 69–70, 94
Charlottesville 25, 55, 63
Chavez, Cesar 95
Chavez, Hugo 2
checks and balances 6–8, 14, 15
Cheney, Liz 43
Christian, Jeremy Joseph 25
Christians, early 46
Cicero, Marcus Tullius 28, 46, 49–50, 53–54, 62, 77–78, 81, 89
Cincinnatus 39–41, 43–44, 82
Cinna, Cornelius 24
citizenship
    Italian allies 23, 34, 35
    Roman 23, 33–34
    US 35, 36
civic virtue 3, 7, 11, 18, 39–44, 51, 89
Civil Rights Act 47
civil rights movement 15, 91
civil strife 5, 7, 8, 11, 18, 23, 24, 41, 83
Civil War, US 15
Claudius Marcellus, Gaius 66
Cleon 45
Cleopatra 82, 83
climate crisis 68, 76, 94
Clinton, Bill 11, 79
Clinton, Hillary 51, 84
Clodius Pulcher, Publius 54, 61–62, 77
Cloelia xvi, 97n4
Clyde, Andrew S. 43
collegia 61
Columbine shooting 63
common good xvi, 3, 9, 13–15, 17, 18, 22, 28, 34, 37, 39, 57, 59, 66, 68, 74, 79, 94
Congress 8, 31, 42, 51, 55, 66, 67, 70, 79
    reconciliation process 67
Constitution, US xvi, 7, 8, 15, 35, 50–52, 76, 78, 91
consulship 10, 27–29, 57, 58, 69, 78, 86
coronavirus. *See* pandemic
coup, US. *See* Capitol insurrection
COVID-19. *See* pandemic

Crassus, Marcus Licinius 46, 57–59, 62, 70
Cremutius Cordus, Aulus 89
Crusius, Patrick 25
Cruz, Ted 55
Curiel, Gonzalo 83
Curio, Gaius Scribonius 66

debt ceiling 66
Declaration of Independence 91
Declaration of Sentiments xvi
democracy 6, 8, 11, 15, 16, 24, 47, 50, 67, 76, 94
    direct xvi
Democratic Party 8, 31, 36, 51
Department of Justice 70, 71
Dershowitz, Alan 52
dictatorship, Roman 39–41, 44, 47, 49
Dio Cassius 90
dominatio (domination) 13–16, 85
Domitian 90
Donations of Alexandria 82
Drusus, Marcus Livius 24, 34
Duterte, Rodrigo 30

economic inequality 2, 7, 17–20, 25, 39, 49, 60, 68, 76, 83, 91, 93, 94
El Paso shooting 25, 55
elections, Roman 2, 5, 14, 29, 49–52, 62, 81, 86, 89–90
    bribery 49, 50, 65
    violence 62, 64, 65
elections, US 24, 41–44, 50–52, 75, 76, 79
    2000 50, 74–75, 83
    2016 11, 30, 50–52, 75, 84, 86–87
    2020 8, 11, 30, 35, 41–44, 50–52, 63, 64, 71, 79
    Arizona 52
    Georgia 35, 51, 52, 71
    right to vote 35
    violence 10–11, 24–25, 30, 41–43, 47, 51, 52, 55, 62–64, 75–76, 94
Electoral College 50, 51
Emerson, Ralph Waldo 75
Erdogan, Recep Tayyip 30
Eunus 45
Europe 1, 45, 78, 91
    and Roman slavery 45–46
exceptionalism, American 7

INDEX

fake news 79
fall of Rome xv
Fields, James 25
filibuster 11, 67, 117n4
Final Decree (*Senatus Consultum Ultimum*) 23, 29, 53
First Triumvirate 57
Flag Officers 4 America 31
flattery. *See* servility
Fletcher, Micah 25
Florence 2
Floyd, George 31, 76
forbearance 23, 39, 44, 95
Founders, US 1, 15, 41
freedom of speech 77–79, 89–91

Galicia, Francisco 36
Garland, Merrick 11
gerrymandering 50
Gianforte, Greg 79
Gibbon, Edward xv
Gini coefficient 18, 19
Giuliani, Rudy 71, 75
Glaucia, Gaius Servilius 29
Goodman, Eugene 43
government shutdowns 66
Gracchus, Gaius 21, 23, 34, 53
Gracchus, Tiberius 9, 21–24, 49, 61, 90
Graham, Lindsey 51
grain distribution, Roman 23, 40
Great Recession 18, 83
Greece 17, 22, 45, 83
Gregory of Nyssa 110n7
gun violence 25, 63, 75

Harmodius 73
Hipparchus 73
Hirtius, Aulus 78
Hitler, Adolf 2
human trafficking 1, 47
Hussein, Saddam 60
Hyer, Heather 25, 63

immigration 33–37
   DACA 36
   family separation 36
   Rome 33–35
   and US armed services 36

indigenous peoples 1, 24, 35
individualism 15, 19
institutions, political 2, 5, 8, 65–68
Insurrection Act, 1807 31
Iraq War 42, 59–60, 83
Islamophobia 25
Italy 5, 40, 45, 46, 53, 62, 66

Jacobs, Ben 79
January 6. *See* Capitol insurrection
Jim Crow 24, 47
Judaea, ancient 59
Jugurtha 27, 28
Justinian 67

Kentucky State House protest 63
King Jr., Martin Luther xvi
   "I Have a Dream" speech xvi
   "Letter from Birmingham Jail" 91
Ku Klux Klan 62

labor rights movement 15, 25
labor unions 18–19
Lafayette Square 31, 71
Las Vegas 63
Latin America 36
Lepidus, Marcus Aemilius 78, 82
liberty 2, 13–16, 46, 77, 89–91, 94
   Roman *libertas* 13–14
   United States 15–16
licentia (license) 13
Lincoln Memorial 31
Lincoln, Abraham 16
   Gettysburg Address 91
Livy 9, 18, 40
Long, Huey P. 30
Long, Robert Aaron 25
Lucan 59, 70
Lucretia 2
Lupercalia festival 74
luxury, Roman 17–18, 40

Madison, James 97n3
Maduro, Nicolás 30
magistrates, Roman 5–7, 9, 14, 62
   collegiality 14
   elections 2, 5, 14, 29, 49, 50, 62, 65, 81, 90

Malcolm X 95
Malheur National Wildlife Refuge takeover 63
Mangum, Destinee 25
Marcus Aurelius 67, 90
Marius Gratidianus, Marcus 49
Marius, Gaius 24, 27–30, 49, 57, 61, 86
mask mandates 63, 68
mass incarceration 47
Massingale, Bryan 47
Mattis, James 31
McVeigh, Timothy 11
Mediterranean 2, 5, 17, 18, 33, 57, 70, 90
Metellus Pius Scipio, Quintus 62
Metellus, Quintus 27, 28
Michigan State House protest 68
Middle East 36, 59
  ancient 45
military, US 30–31, 36, 43–44
militias and political gangs 61–64
Miller, Stephen 36
Milo, Titus Annius 61–62
Mithridates 29, 35, 40, 57
mixed constitution 6–7
Modi, Narendra 30
Mohamed, Walia 25
monarchy 2, 6
monarchy, Rome 2, 6, 7, 13
mos maiorum 9
Mother Emanuel A.M.E. shooting 63
Mueller, Robert 51, 70
Mutina 78

Namkai-Meche, Taliesin 25
Native Americans. *See* indigenous peoples
Nero 46, 90
Nixon, Richard 30
North Africa, Roman 17, 22, 27
Numantia 21

Obama, Barack 11, 36, 54, 55, 67, 79
Ocasio-Cortez, Alexandria 43
Octavia 82, 83
Octavian. *See* Augustus
Oklahoma City bombing 11
Omar, Ilhan 37, 84
Opimius, Lucius 23

opioid addiction 19
Orbán, Viktor 30

Pakistan 59
pandemic 15, 18, 19, 36, 47, 52, 67–68, 76, 83, 84
Pansa, Gaius Vibius 78
Parkland 63
Parthia 59, 70, 73
partisanship 7, 8, 31, 50, 65, 66, 69
Paycheck Protection Program 19
Pedanius Secundus 46
Pelosi, Nancy 43
Pence, Mike 43
Pergamum 21
Pharsalus 70
Philippi 10, 81–82, 91
Pinkertons 62–63
Plato 5–6, 15
political norms and transgressions xvi, 10–11
political parties 7, 8, 24
political violence 1–3, 7, 21–25, 39, 61–64, 94
Polybius 5–9, 18, 93
Pompey, Gnaeus 10, 27, 28, 30, 54, 57–59, 61, 62, 65–66, 70, 77, 82, 86
Port Huron Statement, xvi
Principate 97n1
property 18, 22, 24, 28, 43, 81
proscriptions 24, 40, 45, 49, 78, 81
Proud Boys 63–64
Publilius Syrus 14
Pulse nightclub shooting 63
Putin, Vladimir 30

QAnon conspiracy 84

racism 19, 25, 47–48, 76, 91, 93
Raffensperger, Brad 52
Ramos, Jarrod 79
Reagan, Ronald 79
Reconstruction 11
Remus 33
Republican Party 8, 11, 30, 43, 51, 67, 75
republicanism 25, 86, 90–91
res publica. *See* Roman Republic

rex (king) 13
Roman constitution xvi, 10, 49, 53
Roman Empire xv, 5, 10, 21, 33, 34, 89–90, 94, 97n1
Roman military 18, 59
  campaigns abroad 22, 57–59
  conquest 17, 18, 58, 85
  triumph 21, 40, 57–58, 65, 69, 83
Roman people 2, 6, 7, 20, 22, 30, 34, 39, 61, 81, 90
  Italian allies 23, 34–35
Roman Republic xv–xvi, 2, 3, 5–11, 17, 18, 20, 21, 24, 44, 45, 65, 67, 69, 89, 91, 94, 97n1
Romney, Mitt 42
Romulus 33
Roosevelt, Franklin 23
Russia 1–2, 60

Sallust 9, 18, 53
Salvius 45
Sandy Hook 63
Saturninus, Lucius Appuleius 28–29
Scipio Aemilianus 21
Second Triumvirate 81
senate, Rome 6, 7, 10, 11, 14, 21–23, 27, 28, 34, 39, 40, 43, 46, 50, 52–54, 58, 65–67, 69, 75, 77, 78, 81, 83, 85, 89
  senate house 29, 62, 86, 90
Senate, US 11, 43, 67, 75
Seneca 48
September 11, 54, 83
servility 13–14, 89–90
Shakespeare, William 74
Sicily 45, 46
slavery
  Rome 1, 45–46, 89
  US 1, 47, 91
Social War 34–35
Spain, Roman province 17, 21, 22, 45
Spartacus 45–46, 57
Stalin 1, 2
strongman politics 27–31
Suetonius 85, 90
Sulla, Lucius Cornelius 24, 27–30, 40–41, 43–44, 49, 57, 61, 62, 73, 78
Sulpicius Rufus, Publius 29

sumptuary laws, Roman 17–18
Syria, Roman 59

Tacitus 5, 9, 10, 14, 46, 85, 86, 89, 90, 94
Tarquinius Superbus 2, 74
terrorism 54–55, 62–63
Thapsus 70
Thirteenth Amendment 47
Tiber River 17, 21, 23, 40
Tiberius Gemellus 90
Tiberius, emperor 89, 90
Tiro 46
Trajan 90
Tree of Life Synagogue shooting 63
tribune of the plebs 9, 10, 21–23, 27, 28–29, 34, 40, 49, 54, 61, 66, 73, 85–86, 89, 90, 85
Trump, Donald
  Capitol insurrection 25, 30, 41–44, 47, 55, 63–64, 79
  criminal prosecution 70–71
  elections 51–52, 63–64, 71, 74–76
  first impeachment 51, 75
  hyper-masculinity 84
  and immigrants 36–37, 55
  Make America Great Again 86
  and pandemic 36, 47, 52, 67–68, 76, 84
  political norms 10–11
  and political violence 25, 30, 63–64
  and the press 52, 79
  second impeachment 30, 43, 75
  strongman 30–31
  white supremacy 47, 55, 83–84
Tulsa Race Massacre 25
Twelve Tables 17
Twitter 30, 43
tyranny 2, 13–15, 94

USA PATRIOT Act 54

Venice 2
Vergil 33
Vespasian 90
Vindman, Alexander 75
Virginia State House protest 63
Voting Rights Act 47

War on Terror 59–60
Washington, DC 1, 52, 60
Washington, George 23, 41, 95
Watson, Davino 36
Weimar Republic 2
White Americans 25, 76
white privilege 42, 48

white supremacy 47, 55, 94
Whitmer, Gretchen 63
Women, US 15, 35, 79, 84, 95
WTO protests 42

xenophobia 19, 93

www.ingramcontent.com/pod-product-compliance
Lightning Source LLC
Chambersburg PA
CBHW032028230426
43671CB00005B/233